New York's Finest

KS Publications
www.kikiswinson.net

Publisher's address:
K.S. Publications
P.O. Box 68878
Virginia Beach, VA 23471

Website: www.kikiswinson.net

Email: KS.publications@yahoo.com

ISBN-13: 978-0984529063
ISBN-10: 0-984529063

First Edition: October 2011
1098765

Editors: J. Wooden & Letitia Carrington
Interior & Cover Design: Davida Baldwin (Odd-Balldsgn.com)
Cover Photography: Davida Baldwin (OBDPhotography.com)

Don't Miss Out On These Other Titles:

Wifey
I'm Still Wifey
Life After Wifey
Still Wifey Material
Wifey 4-Life
Mad Shambles
The Candy Shop
Still Candy Shopping
A Sticky Situation
Sleeping with the Enemy (with Wahida Clark)
Heist (with De'nesha Diamond)
Playing Dirty
Notorious
Cheaper to Keep Her part 1
Cheaper to Keep Her part 2
Cheaper to Keep Her part 3
Wife Extraordinaire part 1
Wife Extraordinaire Returns part 2
Lifestyles of the Rich and Shameless (with Noire)

PROLOGUE

When I first laid eyes on the Federal Agents who were being accompanied by the airport police, I damn near had a heart attack. They were fifty feet away from me. If I wanted to make my escape, then now was the perfect time. Unfortunately for me, every government agent with a badge and gun had every exit in this entire fucking airport blocked off. So the possibilities of me getting away from law enforcement were *slim to improbable*. And even if they weren't, where would I go?

Immediately after I got word that our entire operation blew up in our faces, we got word that the Feds were about to make their arrests, so I was given instructions to go to my place to clean out my safe, erase my hard-drive on my laptop and get my ass over to the hideaway apartment Reggie and I had across town. It was a place no one knew about but the three of us.

Meanwhile the Feds and the airport police were minutes from closing in on me. I tried to figure out my next step as my heart raced uncontrollably. The edge I had over them was that they were looking for a young woman fitting my description and not a senior citizen woman wearing a grayish colored wig with streaks of black, an old faded blue dress, a pair of orthopedic shoes and walked with a cane. Believe me, I acted the part on queue and used my knowledge of the airport's security system to my advantage. Only a select few of the employees knew the airport was equipped with over a thousand rotating surveillance cameras and fortunately for me, I was one of them. I also knew there were so many cameras that the security staff could not observe them all simultaneously, which immediately prompted me to change my escape plan.

The airport's generator room was only three feet from me. I eased towards the door very carefully. I acted as if I had lost something on the floor and right before I swiped my key card to make my entry, I glanced around the concourse to make sure I was free and clear. When I realized passengers and airline staff had fixed their attention on the manpower search that had engulfed the entire airport, I knew now was the perfect time to make my exit.

Without hesitation, I swiped my key card and pushed the door open. And just when I thought I was about to make a clean getaway, the security alarm went off. Immediately, my body became panic stricken. I didn't know whether to proceed through the door or turn back around. But as soon as I heard several of the law enforcement officers yell from behind me, I instantly looked back and noticed a horde of law enforcement types rapidly rushing towards me. I could tell by the expressions on their faces that they wanted me badly. I slammed the door shut and looked around the machine-filled room for something I could use to barricade the door. My heart beat at an incredible pace as I scanned and moved around the room. Then I finally saw a pipe lying next to one of the big generators. I snatched it up from the floor and said a quiet and quick prayer as I raced back to the door. I heard the commotion on the other side of the door. There were at least two different voices yelling obscenities as they struggled to get the door open.

"Who has a fucking key card?" I heard one officer yell over top of the loud blaring sound of the security alarm.

That question alone gave me a glimmer of hope that I may be able to prevent them from getting into this room. Now I had to hurry and place the pipe between the crease of the metal bar and the floor. So when they tried to push the door open, the pipe wouldn't allow the door to move one inch.

Not even ten seconds after I placed the pipe against the door, I heard a loud booming sound hit the door. BOOM! But the door didn't budge. "On the count of three, let's hit it again," I heard one of the officers yell. On the count of three, I watched nervously as they hit the door again. But the door didn't budge. "She's gotta have something barricading the door," I heard another male's voice yell over the top of the continued blaring sounds coming from the alarm system.

Knowing that they had figured out what I had done sent my mind into overdrive. I knew I had very limited time to find my way out of this room before they found a way inside. I had to get a move on it if I wanted to escape this madness.

When I turned around to bolt into the opposite direction, I was stopped in my tracks by a police-issued .40 caliber Glock.

"Where the fuck you think you're going?" said a man's voice as he pointed his pistol directly in my face.

The words *slim to improbable* reverberated throughout my mind as I looked down the biggest barrel I had ever been face-to-face with.

NEW YORK'S FINEST

CHAPTER 1

Internationally Known

I was elated when the pilot finally landed our aircraft. We had been in the air for five and a half damn hours. The flights from San Diego to LaGuardia were always long and hard on my stomach. Having worked for the airlines for a little over five years, you would think I would be used to it by now. But unfortunately I wasn't.

What I had gotten used to were the perks of being a flight attendant. A lot of my co-workers weren't aware of it, but I was *New York's Finest.* I was a fly chick from Harlem and I was very popular amongst the men who were elite members of the airline and flew first class. I had them eating out of my fucking hands.

To get straight to the point, I'd befriended and fucked most of them. In return, they'd give me monetary gifts as well as expensive gold and diamond jewelry. Some would say I was being the typical flight attendant, fucking a passenger on every flight. But there was nothing atypical about what I was doing. I didn't consider myself a whore, but this pussy wasn't cheap; hence, the gold and diamond pussy. But the best connections I scored were three passengers who had lucrative drug connections. Unfortunately, after several deals, only one outlasted the other two. His name was Juan Alvarez.

Alvarez was from Costa Rica but he owned a lot of prime real estate here in New York. Not only did he have plenty of money, he had sex appeal. We dated for a few months. During that time I introduced him to my brother, Reggie. Alvarez and Reggie hit if off well and from there, we started a moneymaking enterprise that couldn't be tampered with. While I needed to make more money than the measly $17 an hour I was receiving from the airlines, Reggie needed a consistent supplier and Juan needed someone to put his coke on the streets. So it became a win-win situation for everyone involved.

Alvarez was a womanizer and when I learned that, I cut our relationship short. But we didn't end our business relationship. In the world we both grew up in, money talked and bullshit walked. Juan, Reggie and I had a good business venture, and more importantly, we had a means of transport—my flights to and fro locations across the globe. And as long as I had my bag handlers, TSA agents and mules help get Juan's coke through the airports, he promised he'd continue to supply Reggie and then we all would be happy.

After all the passengers exited our aircraft, my fellow flight attendants, Brooke and Kelsey, inspected the aisles and seats to ensure passengers hadn't left any of their belongings behind. Once that task was completed, we exited the plane ourselves.

I retrieved my Blackberry from my carry-on bag as I entered the airport and called Reggie. I had his number on speed dial, so it only took a matter of seconds to get him on the line.

"What's good?" he asked. He sounded very excited to hear from me. As a matter of fact, he'd always got excited when I called him after I came in from a flight. He knew that once he heard my voice, I had some high quality product coming his way.

"I hear the cheer in your voice," I told him.

"You damn right! When I hear your voice it makes me happy. Not only do I know that you're home safe, I also know that you've brought home some shit that's going to make us richer than we were yesterday."

I chuckled at Reggie's comment. He was a comedian in his own right. But he was better at selling coke. I introduced Juan to Reggie six months ago and since then, Reggie and I have generated a large sum of cash. I can't count Reggie's money, but I can say that I had saved over two million dollars. I thought about quitting my job as a flight attendant several times, but Reggie stressed over a dozen times how he needed someone on the inside to watch over his investments. He figured that if I left the airline, then he wouldn't have a set of trusting eyes watching to make sure his packages arrived safely into New York. So that's one of the reasons why I was still employed.

"Where are you?" I asked.

"I'm cross town at Malika's apartment. But I'm about to head back uptown because Vanessa's been ringing my Blackberry off the fucking hook. I told her I was out handling business but for some reason she doesn't believe me."

I chuckled once again. "Come on Reggie, are you listening to yourself? You've cheated on her over a dozen times since you two have been married, so ask yourself why should she believe you?"

He totally ignored my question. The only thing he wanted to talk about was how pure his coke was and how much money he stood to make. And immediately after I gave him the numbers we ended our conversation. Before we hung up, I assured him I would go to the TSA office to check up on the bags to make sure they hadn't been tampered with. And then I'd put them in the right hands, so he could get them before nightfall.

I had had a long day, but when I looked at how much I had accomplished, I felt good. Normally when I came home from a long flight, I'd take a hot shower and then I'd slip into my terrycloth pajamas and watch a couple of Blue Ray movies. Tonight, I decided to order Chinese and then hit the sack.

While I waited for my Chinese food to be delivered, I got a phone call from my sister-in-law, Vanessa. From time to time she'd pick up the phone to call me when she needed advice on how to handle certain situations with Reggie. I pretty much listened to her take on things, but at the end of the day my allegiance was with my brother. I would never sell him out even if he were wrong. He was my blood. And whether Vanessa realized it by now, Reggie was going to do what the fuck he wanted and when he wanted, and there's nothing she or I could do to change that.

Reggie has been and always will be a fucking street hustler. Our father was a street cat, so hustling ran through our blood strong. Reggie had stepped the game up big time. He excelled as an athlete in high school—the star running back on our football team and the point guard in basketball. Even then he was a hustler. He ran a betting racket on the football and basketball games he played in. Amazingly, as teenagers we were raking in bags of dough. As the dude setting the line, and the athlete controlling the results, we always won both on the field and in the streets. And it all computed to one thing—mo' money, mo' money. And that's some real shit!

"Naomi, you need to talk to your brother before I get his ass locked up!" she yelled. Her tone was sharp and I could tell that she was extremely angry. I could also tell that she was pacing the floor in their one million dollar home. She was known for rocking four and a half inch Giuseppe Zanotti heels, so I'd bet money that those were the shoes she rattled the floor with.

"What's wrong? And where is he?" I asked, even though I sensed things were a bit chaotic on the other end of the telephone receiver.

"I'm about to call the motherfucking police on his ass if he puts his hands on me again," she continued to roar.

Before I made one comment, I shook my head with disgust, because there was no doubt in my mind that she ignited this feud with my brother. Vanessa was a fucking drama queen. If the world didn't revolve around her ass, then all hell would break loose. Granted, she was gorgeous and fly. In fact, she looked like a pretty, big booty, small waist chick from Brazil. But Reggie pulled this chick straight out of one of those projects from Jersey, put her in their luxury, two-bedroom high-rise apartment, laced her with a wardrobe of high-end designers and just recently purchased her a white four door late model Jaguar with white leather interior. She was the envy of all the chicks from her old neighborhood. However, if they knew everything she had came with a price, they'd switch their focus on something else.

Unfortunately for Reggie, he and Vanessa had been together for close to four years, so he'd have to kill her to get rid of her silly ass. She came into his life when Reggie banked his first million. I'd always believed that timing was everything, so she could not have picked a better time to come into his life.

"Vanessa, put him on the phone," I instructed her because it didn't matter how mad and upset my brother was, I knew how to calm him down. It took him a few seconds to get on the line but as soon as I heard him ask me what was up, I came back with my own question. "Reggie, what is going on around there?"

"I'm about to kill this bitch! That's what's going on!" he snapped.

"Reggie, can you calm the fuck down? You got too much shit to handle tonight. So if you put your hands on Vanessa, she might just call your bluff and dial 911 on your ass this time around. And if she does that, then you won't be able to handle your affairs behind bars."

"The day she calls the police on me is the day she's getting the fuck out of here," he roared in return.

"I know that. And I'm sure she does too, but tonight isn't a good night to be testing the waters. There's a lot of money to be made before sunrise so leave that bullshit alone and get the fuck out of there," I advised him.

"I'm getting ready to leave right now," he told me.

I could tell he was moving through the house, so I was beginning to feel a little at ease. Reggie had just scored a boat load of coke. This package was the come up for the both of us. It was pure as pure can get. And the fact that we got it for a good price made our profit margin skyrocket. See, not only was I a flight attendant, I was also an opportunist. I'd only fuck with you or do something for you, if there's something in it for me. A lot of people don't like it, but that's their business. This was my life and I chose to live it the way I wanted.

Marco Chavez, who was Reggie's and mine current coke supplier, lived by this same philosophy. In the beginning, I had no idea that he was a coke dealer when I met him on one of our flights from Miami. He had the appearance of a rich real estate investor or a nightclub owner, so money was written all over him. He took my number and the rest was history. That was over a year and a half ago and even though we're no longer fucking, we still had a good working relationship, which was how I intended to keep it.

When money is involved in any situation, you have to put your feelings in your pocket and make the right choice. I learned a long time ago from both my pops and my brother that the only way a woman could survive in this world was if she didn't make decisions based on her emotions. You see men are logical, don't get into that bullshit. They come up with a plan and then they execute it. Reggie was known for taking a couple of days to make final decisions. And lately, I've adapted that same method, along with a few others.

When Reggie finally made it out to his car, I let out a sigh of relief because I knew he was about to make his move. "Do you think you're gonna need me to come out to the spot with you?" I asked him after I heard the car door close.

"Nah, I'm straight. Me and Damian will be able to handle everything," he assured me.

"Well, if you need me, just pick up the phone."

"A'ight," he said and then he hung up.

Chapter 2

My Day Off

Normally on my day off I'd lounge around my apartment and catch up on some previously recorded reality shows. But since there was money that needed to be picked up from a few of Reggie's spots, I slipped into a pair of blue denim shorts and accented it with my *I'm Proud to be a Puerto Rican* t-shirt, although I'm half black as well. I topped it off with a cute pair of old school Adidas sneakers. Every now and again, I'd go back to my roots and get into my 'hood wear.

On a more serious note, I had to fit the part when I rolled out to Reggie's spots to handle my business. Mostly everyone in the 'hood knew me, but that's not who I was worried about. From time to time, the narcotics detectives would bribe their way into the apartment of one of the elderly tenants in the buildings of the project and set up surveillance operations. So if I ever went there looking as if I didn't belong, then I'd immediately become their next target. And I can't have that. I had invested too much into our operation to have one slip up such as that fuck up everything. And it was equally important because one day very soon I had planned to take all the money I had saved and leave the country for good.

On my way out of my luxury apartment, I grabbed my keys, my Yves Saint Laurent sunshades and handbag, and marched on to the elevator. Down in the lobby area of my building, the doorman saw me approaching the exit door and rushed to open it.

"How are you doing this morning Ms. Foxx?" he asked.

"I'm doing great Sam. Thanks for asking," I replied as I made my way out of the building. Like clockwork, my vehicle was parked out front and ready for me to get on the road.

I'm a huge fan of Lil Wayne, so I hit the power button for my eight disc CD player and turned up the volume on *How To Love.* The hook on this track had my head rocking from one side to the next. And when it ended I hit the repeat button and listened to it three more times until I got to my destination, which was Harlem, my old stomping grounds. The block surrounding the Polo Grounds was crowded with cats trying to get their paper. I recognized a few of the locals and smiled at them after I exited my car.

"Can you keep an eye out for my baby?" I asked no one in particular, referring to my new midnight black Mercedes GL550 SUV.

"You know we gotcha' ma," I heard one of the guys say. I couldn't call any names, but I knew their faces all too well. And they knew me, which was what counted most. They also knew that I wasn't to be fucked with. Being a Foxx gave me recognition and status, which meant I could leave the car running and no one would touch it. My brother Reggie laid down the law from day one and every one of these cats who patrolled the Polo Grounds knew the consequences if his law was broken. I was certainly off limits. No one could harm one little hair on my sweet ass body. Not too mention they also had to ensure no one else from the outside of this compound fucked with me, my whip or anything I was transporting. Or they had hell to pay.

The compound consisted of four buildings that we called the Four Towers. The Towers had been there ever since I could remember. As a child, my mother and hustler father used to warn us about hanging out at the Towers. It was where the action was, and that action at some point over time had moved from one tower to the next.

After one of the guys assured me I had nothing to worry about, I proceeded to make my rounds. The first stop was to this chick's apartment that was in first tower. Her name was Candie and she lived on the sixth floor. When I entered the lobby, I was met by two of Reggie's marksmen, or shall I say the lookout patrol. Each building had its own lookout patrol. Ben and Dre' were both big guys standing around six feet tall and not easy on the eyes. But who cared how they looked, they weren't paid to stand around and look pretty. Their job was to make sure no one came into the building that shouldn't be there while I made my rounds. Reggie made sure his men were fully armed with heavy artillery when I entered into each of the four towers. And after I made my presence known, they greeted me and moved out of the way.

"Be back in a minute," I told them and then I headed for the elevator. I was lucky the elevator was working. Most times the elevator would be out, and I hated those days when they came. I was in excellent shape and did my share of walking getting from point A to point B in the numerous airports I had traveled through. But walking up six, seven or ten flights of stairs was not my idea of fun or staying in shape.

As I approached the elevator door, it opened and out came a very familiar face. This familiar face was Angel. Angel was a chick Reggie once used to hold his dope packages until she messed around and allowed her twenty-year-old baby brother to steal several grams out of each package so they could sell it to make an extra profit. When Reggie found out about it, he made sure her brother never walked again and she only walked with one arm. Thank God he listened to me and didn't have them killed. He did make an example out of them though. After I smiled and said hello, I continued onto the elevator.

When I reached the sixth floor, I was met by two more of Reggie's patrolmen. Lucky, the patrolman I was very familiar with held the elevator door open as I stepped out into the hallway. Then he prevented the elevator door from closing to prevent anyone else from getting on the elevator. This was a precautionary measure Reggie instructed them to take to protect me and isolate me from riding in the elevator with anyone else while I made my rounds to pick up his dough. You never know if he had enemies out to interrupt his business or worse, hurt someone close to him—namely me. So far it had worked as advertised.

"Lucky, you look like you're working hard?" I commented.

"Most definitely. I do this all day, every day," he smiled. Reggie gave him the name Lucky because his short ass had been shot twice and both times he escaped death. Now he had a metal plate in the back of his head. Although he pretended the plate didn't bother him, I knew it did. I had caught him go into a zone. His eyes would glaze over and you could tell he was in another world. And during this time, he would go the fuck off, most times for no reason at all. I witnessed him beat the hell out of his babymama for no reason. It's rumored that he received a disability check every month for his condition. So regardless of his short height, a lot of cats out here didn't fuck with Lucky. We all knew he really was certified crazy.

The other brother was Walter, Walt for short. Reggie had just put him on the payroll, so he was new to our team. He was kind of cute, and he was definitely my type. But he was the help. And I didn't fuck the help. Equally, and probably more importantly, Reggie didn't play that. Too bad for Walt, because we probably would've made some serious chemistry in my king-size slay bed.

Like clockwork, as soon as I knocked, Candie opened the door to let me in, then she closed the door behind me. We proceeded directly to the kitchen of her small apartment and she handed me a manila envelope filled with cash. Different day, same procedure every time.

"It's all there," she assured me.

"I'm sure it is. But you know I always count the money in front of you just so we can be on the same page. But when you tell me that everything is here and then I go behind you and find out that you are short, then that's not a good look."

"I understand," she replied in her childlike voice.

Candie wasn't your typical ghetto chick. She was a very pretty Puerto Rican, a mother of one, who spoke very good English, and she was very ambitious. With a five-year-old son, she managed to find a way to hustle for Reggie during the wee hours of the night and pursue her Bachelor's degree in marketing doing the day. I was shocked when I entered her place over a year ago and noticed she was doing homework. It completely blew me away. And from that day on, I had mad respect for this chick. She was a twenty-four year old mother handling her business, who also had plans to pursue her Master's degree. From previous conversations, I knew she was saving money so she could move out of this place and give her and her son a better quality of life. She was all right in my book.

After I finished counting the money, I winked at her and said, "You're right. It's all here."

She smiled back and said, "I told you so." She escorted me back to her front door and I stuffed the envelope inside my handbag before I made my exit. I never left out of anyone's apartment with the money in my hands. That's a big no-no. After I reentered the hallway, Lucky was front and center while Walt stood by the elevator with his hands holding both sides of the sliding doors.

"You a'ight?" Lucky asked.

"Yeah, I'm cool," I replied.

"You ready for me to escort you back downstairs?"

"I'm ready as ever."

"Well, let's do it then," Lucky smiled as he walked alongside of me towards the elevator. Walt held both doors of the elevator open until Lucky and I were safely inside. Once inside, Lucky assured him that he'd be right back as the doors closed.

Lucky pressed the button for the first floor and I actually admired the seriousness in his face. He took his job to heart. I was his mission for now and I felt safe in the elevator with Lucky.

When the top door of the elevator was snatched open and two masked men jump down inside of the elevator, one after the other, tumbling down on top of Lucky, I damn near pissed myself. We were both caught off guard. I screamed as loud as I could and got hit in the mouth with the butt of one of the guy's pistols. I fell hard against the elevator wall.

"Stop the elevator," one guy instructed the other, as he took Lucky's Glock from him. I looked down at poor Lucky. He was knocked the fuck out. I was all alone in this fucking elevator with these two motherfuckers and had no idea what was about to happen next.

They managed to stop the elevator on the third floor. And before I could blink an eye, the guy who snatched Lucky's gun from him, pointed the exact same gun in my face and demanded that I give him the money I had just picked up from Candie's crib. So without hesitation I handed him the manila envelope and begged him to let me live.

"Oh, you don't have to worry about that. I'm gonna let you live this time. But the next time you might not be so lucky," he said. Then he did the unbelievable, he aimed Lucky's gun at him and shot him directly in his face. His entire head blew up like a fucking melon. Blood splattered all over me and the walls of the elevator. And as I began to scream once again, that's when both men fled off the elevator.

I swear, I had never been that afraid in my life. Fear had gripped my whole body. I was afraid to move one inch. I wanted to get up and press the button to close the elevator door but my entire body was paralyzed. And all I could do was cry as I watched Lucky's head ooze blood onto the floor around him. I couldn't believe I had just witnessed Lucky get killed just like that. He and I were just talking a few minutes before all this shit went down and now he's dead.

Oh my God! What am I going to tell Reggie? And the police for that matter. I knew they're going to question me like I was an accomplice. I just hoped that whatever they decided to do, they didn't put my name in the fucking local new papers or mention it to the media that I was in the center of this murder investigation. This wouldn't look good for my employers at the airline. They wouldn't understand why I was out here at the Polo Grounds. Everyone in the state of New York knew the reputation of the Polo Grounds.

That thought, thinking about the airline and my possible firing and overall humiliation brought me back to life. The best way for me to avoid all of the unnecessary drama and publicity was to get a grip and woman up. I wiped my fucking tears, and got the hell off the floor. My mind was on cops and homicide detectives arriving before I could get the fuck out of there. I tried my best not to touch anything. I literally lifted myself from the floor without using my hands and then I used my elbow to press the first floor button.

Then came the waiting—I swear it felt as if the elevator was taking forever to get to the first floor. When it finally stopped and the doors opened, I burst out of the elevator like I was in serious need of some oxygen. Both Ben and Dre rushed towards me.

"What the fuck happened? You been shot?" Dre wondered aloud.

I tried to hold back my tears but the flood gates to my ducts burst out. "No, I didn't get shot. This is Lucky's blood. He was shot in the head by two guys with masks," I sobbed.

Ben rushed over to look inside the elevator. "Oh shit! She ain't lying. That nigga Lucky's brains is hanging out of his fucking head!" Ben replied, hysterically.

Dre left my side and rushed to the elevator to see Lucky's dead body for himself.

I stood there helplessly. I didn't know whether I was coming or going. All I wanted to do was get out of there.

"Who did this shit to him?" Dre rushed back and asked me. I could tell that he was ready to make the guy who did this pay.

"I don't know. They both wore black ski masks," I continued to sob.

"Where did they come from?" Ben wanted to know.

"They were on the roof of the elevator. And as soon as we got on the fifth floor, they busted from the door, robbed me for the money I got from Candie, killed Lucky and then they stopped the elevator on the third floor and ran off," I explained.

"Where is Walt?" Ben asked.

"He's still on the sixth floor, I think."

Ben looked at Dre. "Cover her up and take her to her truck and then call Reggie, while I run upstairs to the sixth floor to see where that nigga Walt, is," he instructed Dre.

"A'ight," Dre said as he moved towards my truck.

Chapter 3

A Bloody Situation

On our way to my truck, Dre got Reggie on the phone so I could talk to him. I briefly explained what happened without saying a whole lot over the phone. And then I told him I couldn't go home the way I was, so he instructed me to meet him at our secret spot on the other side of the Hudson River.

When it was time for me to get into my truck, I hesitated to get inside with my now bloody clothes on. I couldn't afford to get any of Lucky's blood inside of my truck so it could come back and bite my ass later. What the cops could get from DNA was amazing today. But then I figured how would homicide detectives know I was here and to check my truck for traces of his blood if they didn't know I was even here in the first place. So I took a chance and got into my ride and got the hell out of there.

I drove in silence, even turning the radio off, until I got to the destination where Reggie told me to meet him. My nerves were all over the fucking place. I couldn't believe I had just witnessed Lucky get his head blown off. After all this time he'd work for Reggie, he always was able to walk away from death. But today, God had other plans for him. Damn! I wished I had not been there to witness his death, because he was like a little brother to Reggie and I. And even though he hadn't been working for us that long, we had that brotherly thing going on. He was the type of cat that would literally give you the shirt off his back if you needed it. He was definitely a ride or die type of nigga. And as I thought about how this would affect his loved ones, my nerves became more frayed. I was one thought away from becoming an emotional wreck. And the only thing that would calm me down was my brother. So I pressed down on the accelerator and maneuvered through all the busy traffic in Harlem to get to him.

When I pulled up to Reggie's hideaway spot across town, he and Damian were outside waiting for me. I exhaled when I saw their faces. I don't remember putting my truck in park, but I do remember how it felt to be in my brother's arms. He was like my savior and with him I knew he'd protect me from this point on.

As tears started falling again, I became choked up. In a matter of thirty seconds, I had his shirt soaked and wet. I couldn't talk to save my life. And when he realized I needed to calm down, he instructed Damian to help him take me inside. Inside of Reggie's home away from home, which was the place he came when Vanessa got on his fucking nerves, he led me towards the bathroom.

"We need to get you out of these clothes," Reggie told me.

I nodded my head and allowed him to escort me down the hallway. As he led the way, I realized I was going to be okay. I was in his safe house. This apartment was like his sanctuary. No one knew about it but the three of us. And anytime he'd tell Vanessa he was out of town, nine times out of ten he'd come here for a little R and R. You would think that since his own wife didn't know about this spot, he'd bring his mistresses or side chicks here. But no way, he didn't play that. He kept most of his money stashed away in this apartment, so he wouldn't play himself. If he wanted some new pussy, he would take one of those hoes to the nearest hotel. No ifs, ands or buts about it.

After Reggie left the bathroom, I closed the door behind him, got undressed and jumped into the shower. It didn't take me long at all to get all of Lucky's blood off of me. When I jumped out of the shower, I wrapped myself inside one of the big oversized towels hanging up and exited the bathroom.

"Your things are in the other bedroom," Reggie yelled from the living room. I knew what he was talking about. About a year ago, Reggie and I thought it would be necessary for us to have an emergency bag filled with a couple pairs of changing clothes, travel credentials such as a fake identification card, passport and as much cash as we could take. I went into the bedroom to retrieve the carry-on bag from the floor of the walk-in closet.

After I slipped on one of the outfits I had tucked away in my emergency travel bag, I joined Reggie and his right hand man, Damian, in the living room. Reggie was on the phone when I walked in, so I took a seat on the sofa next to Damian. He looked at me from head to toe. Then he placed his left arm around my shoulder.

"Are you feeling a little better?" he asked.

"I'm still a little bit shaken up but I'll be alright," I assured him.

"A'ight, well hurry up and see what you can find out," I heard Reggie bark on the phone. "I want to know who the triggerman was and the nigga who was with him. Oh yeah, don't let that nigga, Walt, go nowhere until I get there. As a matter of fact, take him to Monty's girl's crib and keep an eye out on him, because this shit needs to be handled before the sun comes up tomorrow."

I knew Reggie was beyond furious about this whole thing. Not only had I witnessed one of his soldiers getting murdered, I was caught up in the middle of the crossfire and I was robbed in the process. So I knew that whoever was responsible was going to die a very slow death when it was all said and done.

As soon as he ended his call, Reggie took a seat in the chair directly across from me and leaned in towards me. "How you feeling?" he didn't hesitate to ask.

I let out a long sigh. "I'm better than I was an hour ago," I told him.

"Do you feel like talking about what happened?"

As bad as I wanted to tell him no and I preferred to forget about what happened, I knew that he wouldn't be too happy. At the end of the day, all he wanted was to get to the bottom of the murder and robbery, and find who had the audacity to put me in harm's way. And if I could give him any information that would help him find the fucking culprits, then he'd be the happiest man on earth.

"Look, if you don't want to tell the whole story, just tell me what happened right after you left Candie's apartment," Reggie said.

I took a deep breath and then I exhaled, while both Reggie and Damian gave me their undivided attention. "Right after I stuck the money Candie gave me in my handbag, I left the apartment and met Lucky by the elevator. Everything was cool. Nothing seemed strange or out of the ordinary, so when he and I got onto the elevator we went with the flow of things. And when the two guys jumped down into the elevator while we were passing the fifth and fourth floors, we were caught off guard. It was like, Lucky didn't have no time at all to shoot or stop them from coming down on us. I mean, they knocked him completely out within a few seconds."

"So they hit Lucky before he could react and I see they hit you too," Reggie noticed as he zoomed in on my face.

Unconsciously, I massaged the area of my face where I was hit while Reggie stared at it. "It hurt like hell after the guy hit me, but it's not that bad now," I told him.

"Dre told me dude said something to you before he shot Lucky," Reggie probed for more information.

"Yeah, after the guy took the money from me, I begged him not to kill me. So after he told me he wasn't going to do it this time, he looked back over at Lucky and killed him instead, while the other guy played look out."

"What did they do after that?"

"They ran out of the elevator."

"Did you see which way they ran?" Reggie continued his questions.

The questions upset me. Did he really think I would go behind two killers to figure out which way they ran? I mean, I was damn near traumatized by the fact I had just saw a man get his fucking head blown off and that I could've very well had gotten my head blown off too. "Hell no! After they ran out of the elevator, I got up just enough nerves to close the elevator door and pressed the first floor button so I could get out of there!" I snapped.

"Calm down Naomi," Damian said in a soothing voice. "He just wanted to know if there was a chance that you saw something other than what you mentioned to Dre."

I looked back at Damian. "Trust me, if I saw where they went, that would've been the first thing I told Dre when I saw him."

Damian massaged my back in a circular motion. "It's gonna be alright. We gon' take care of those niggas who did this shit to you and Lucky."

"You damn right! Those niggas are going to pay dearly!" Reggie blurted out. "And as soon as I find out who they are and where their families live, I'm going to kill everybody in the fucking crib! No one will leave out of there alive. And that's my motherfucking word. Nobody puts their hands on my fucking sister, kill one of my soldiers and take my motherfucking dough and is able to walk around to talk about it. Fuck nah! That's just not going to happen to me."

I felt the rage in Reggie's voice. He was on a warpath and no one would be able to bring him out of that spell but himself. Damian continued to comfort me after Reggie stormed out of the room. "Do you think you'll be able to drive home?" he asked me.

"I'm not sure," I replied.

"Well, if you want me and Reggie to drop you off, then we'll do that. But you gotta let us know, because as soon as we get the call that the police got the coroner to move Lucky's body out of the elevator and clear the building out, then we gon' head out there so we can have a sit down with Walt."

"A'ight. I'll let y'all know before y'all leave," I told him. And then I laid my head back against the chair.

I hadn't realized I had dozed off until Damian tapped me on my shoulder. "We're getting ready to leave, so if you want us to drop you off, then get ready because we're gonna be leaving in about ten minutes."

I lifted my head to see the clock on the wall. When I realized I had been asleep for two hours I sat up instantly. I knew I had to get up early in the morning to meet my crew for a six a.m. flight to New Orleans. Very seldom I called in sick. My supervisor was a total bitch when she got calls from her flight attendants wanting to take out. If we didn't show up for work it better be because we were in the hospital or dead. Otherwise, you'd better be on the flight assigned to you. And since I didn't need the drama or the headache of being put with another crew, which, of course, would alter my normal pick up route for our product deliveries, I stood up from the sofa.

"I'll leave with you guys, but I want to take my truck with me," I told him.

"You're gonna drive?" Damian asked me.

"Nah, I want you to drive my truck and I'll ride with Reggie."

"A'ight. Cool," he said.

Chapter 4

The Time Has Come

I hopped in Reggie's all black, tinted windowed Suburban while Damian followed us in my truck. Since I had been in his company we hadn't had any time alone to talk about everything that happened earlier. I could tell that he was in deep thought from the moment we left his apartment. "What's on your mind?" I wondered aloud.

He continued to look forward as he maneuvered through the traffic. "I just want some answers when I have this sit down with everybody."

"And what if you don't get the answers you're looking for?" I continued.

"Well, then somebody else is going to pay for what happened today," he replied. As soon as he closed his mouth, I noticed how the veins around his temple started to flair. I figured the more he thought about the possibilities that no one was going to be able to pinpoint who robbed and killed Lucky, the more irrational he'd become. I guessed now would be the perfect time to talk some sense in him. I mean, I was the only person he'd listen to. Not even our father or mother could get through to him when he was about to blow his fucking top.

"Hey, Reggie, I know how badly you want to tear those grimy bastards to shreds, but setting shit off on random motherfuckers ain't gonna get you closer to them," I said after I collected my thoughts. "You're gonna have to think about everything you say and do when you go back out to the Polo Grounds. I mean, you know mad niggas out there got your back, but you're gonna have to come up with a plan."

"Oh, I got a plan," he snapped.

"Calm down, papi. This is me you're talking to. I know how you get down. But remember we got a lot of shit cooking right now and we can't afford to fuck it up behind this shit that happened today. Let's just see what everybody got to say. And then you take it from there."

Reggie looked at the driver side window and then he looked into his rearview window. "You think that nigga, Walt, had something to do with it?" he asked me.

I really wasn't shocked by his question. As long as I've known my brother, he doesn't trust a soul but me. He's paranoid of everyone. "I can't say," I answered him as I thought back on the things that transpired before the actual robbery took place. "It's kind of hard to say because he didn't act any different from any other time I'd seen him."

"Well, he may not have acted any different but he's gonna have a lot of questions to answer. I might even throw Damian on the hot seat too. He did bring that nigga into the fold," Reggie huffed.

"Come on now, you don't think Damian had something to do with this?"

"I don't put shit pass no man. That nigga eat and shit just like I do, so he's just as suspect as that nigga, Walt. But I'll tell you what, somebody better tell me something tonight."

"Just be easy Reggie. I can't tell you enough about how much shit we just got in that needs to be worked. So if you fuck around and put down another body, then that's gonna bring more heat on us. We gotta lay low until all the work is gone," I explained to him. Even though he didn't respond back, I knew he heard me. He was a fucking hot head, but he wasn't stupid.

As soon as we pulled up to my building, I kissed Reggie on the cheek and told him I loved him and to call me as soon as he's done with his meeting. He assured me he would.

Right after Damian hopped out of my truck, the valet took it and drove off. So I walked up to him and said, "Please keep a watch out on Reggie. Please make sure he keeps his cool."

Damian kissed me on the cheek and told me he would.

After he got into the truck with Reggie, they drove off and I couldn't help but wonder how things would play out tonight. I wanted so badly to warn Damian that Reggie wanted to blame him for what happened today. But I couldn't betray my brother's trust. That would be the ultimate sin in his eyes. And he'd never forgive me for it. Loyalty was what he expected from me. So to him, me betraying his trust would make me forever dead in his book.

Upstairs in my apartment, I tried to keep myself busy. It was still kind of light outside so I had plenty of time before I called it a night and laid my butt down. I only had one close friend and her name was Sabrina Alvarez. She was a flight attendant just like me and we also worked together. She lived in the Bronx, but she's always on my side of town. She and I'd been friends for about four years now. She's very cool but she's not cool enough for me to let her in on what Reggie and I got going on. Reggie would slit my fucking throat if I pulled her coattail about our operation. He didn't mind if she and I hung out, go shopping or have a few drinks together, but he had forbidden me to tell her any of my business.

Like me, she was very beautiful and a sexy Latina. She's from the Dominican Republic though. And she's a bad bitch when she has to be. She was very fashion conscious. Niggas knew not to come at her unless they're trying to spend some dough. Reggie had also fucked her a couple of times. But guess what? He paid her for her services by flying her to a ski resort in Aspen for five days and took her shopping on top of that. He dropped a minimum of forty grand on a couple pairs of boots, a diamond necklace and a mink jacket. She made him come out of his motherfucking pockets and if it were me, I'd done the same thing.

Since she was the only friend I had at the moment, I got her on the phone so I could take my mind off the shit that was about to go down at the Polo Grounds.

"Hey, Chica," she said as soon as she answered her cell phone.

"What's good babe? Where you at?" I asked her, trying to make small talk.

"At the bodega picking up some milk and a few other things," she replied. "Why, what's up?"

"Nothing. I was just calling you to see what you were doing since I was sitting here bored out of my mind."

"Are you scheduled to work tomorrow?"

"You know I am. Remember we got that early morning flight to New Orleans?"

"Oh yeah, how can I forget that?" she replied sarcastically. "I get so tired of that crazy ass woman when she schedules us for that mess. She does that shit to piss us off."

"Yeah, I know. But just try not to let it get to you. You see I don't pay that shit she does no mind. I just go on about my damn business."

"That shit you're talking is easier said than done," she laughed. "Oh yeah, you heard about that murder that happened today at your old stomping grounds?" she blurted out. I mean, that shit came from out of nowhere. I didn't know whether to lie or tell her the truth. But then a little birdie whispered in my ear and told me to play dumb. The less I acted like I knew, the less she'd ask me questions. And besides, I figured if she heard something, then she'd be able to tell me what the streets were saying.

"Nah, I didn't hear that," I began to lie. "What happen and when did it happen?"

"I saw it on the news earlier. I started to call you to see if you knew who got killed but I got caught up in some other stuff and forgot all about it."

"What did the news journalist say?" my questions continued.

"They didn't say anything really. All they said was that an unidentified young man in his early twenties got shot in the head execution style in the elevator of one of the towers of the Polo Grounds, and if anyone had any information that could lead to the arrest of the triggerman, than to call the hotline."

"They didn't say anything else?"

"They did say that it may be drug related but they weren't for sure," she replied. "Think your brother may have known the guy that got killed?"

"Reggie knows everybody. So it wouldn't surprise me if he did."

"Have you spoken with him today?"

"Yeah. Earlier. But it was this morning."

"Well, I bet if you call him, he'll be able to tell you more information than me or that reporter on TV," she laughed.

"Like I said before, it wouldn't surprise me," I said and then I turned the direction of the conversation. "So what are you going to get into after you leave the store?"

"I'm not sure. I'll probably pick Kennedy up from preschool and drop her off at her daddy's house since we gotta get on that early flight to New Orleans."

"Yeah, that might be your best bet. That way you won't be scrambling in the morning trying to get her situated so you can get to work on time."

"That makes sense. But I'll call you later."

"Do that," I told her. And then we disconnected our lines.

I sat back on my bed and let out a long sigh of relief. Knowing that the news reporter had no knowledge that I had witnessed Lucky get murdered was a stress reliever. One thing I can say about my people at the Polo Grounds was that they definitely knew how to keep their mouths shut. And that was a huge plus in my book.

Chapter 5

Checking In

I had let a few hours roll by and when I hadn't heard from Reggie I became worried. I knew I wouldn't be able to go to sleep until I knew what had happened at the Polo Grounds.

While I was snuggled in my bed, I grabbed my Blackberry from my nightstand and called Reggie's phone. It rung five times before it went to voicemail. The fact he didn't answer sent me into a state of panic. I tried his number again but got the same results, so I hung up and immediately called Damian's phone. I let out a long sigh of relief when he answered.

"What's up?" he asked. Before I could answer him, I was interrupted by all of the commotion in the background.

"Nigga, you think I'm playing wit' your mother-fucking ass? I will kill you right now. I ain't got no love for niggas who ain't got love for me!" I heard my brother yelling.

His rage was bursting through the roof. I wasn't in the same room with him but there was no doubt in my mind that he had a gun in his hand while he was on this rampage.

"Naomi, you still up here?" Damian asked.

"Yeah, I'm still here," I finally replied. "I just tried to call Reggie's phone twice but he didn't answer it."

"Oh . . . that was you? Yeah, I heard it ring. He picked it up and looked at it but you knew he wasn't going to answer it while he's trying to handle this situation."

"I kind of figured that. Was everything cleaned up when y'all got there?"

"Yeah, it was. But you could still tell something happened."

"Did they seal off the elevator?" I asked.

"Yeah, we heard they ain't letting nobody use it for the next couple of days," Damian spoke low, but audible.

"Did y'all find out who those guys were?"

"Nah, not yet."

"Did your people have any answers for y'all when you guys saw him?"

"He had a few. But it wasn't good enough for your brother," he continued in a low tone.

But you could still hear Reggie laying down the law in the background. "I will not allow a nigga to fuck up my operation. I don't give a fuck who it is. I have taken a lot of risks to let some grimy ass low-level niggas destroy what I built. So if I ever find out one of y'all niggas was behind this shit that happened today, it ain't gon' be pretty for you, your babymamas, your kids and the rest of your motherfucking families. Y'all catch my drift?"

I heard everyone say yeah in unison. And then it got quiet but it didn't stay quiet for long. A second later, I heard Reggie say, "Who the fuck you on the phone with?" Then there was a long pause, but I knew he was talking to Damian.

"It's your sister. She said she just tried to call you."

"Nigga, you were supposed to be watching my back and now you on the motherfucking phone!" I heard Reggie spat. "Shit, if you wanna know the truth, I believe that if you would not have brought this nigga into my operation, then this shit probably wouldn't have happened. So I might have just cause to blame you for this shit, huh?"

"What the fuck are you talking about Reggie? So you think I was behind this shit?" I heard Damian say.

While I waited for my brother to respond, my heart raced at sixty miles per second. I wished like hell I was there to shut this discussion down. Reggie knew he had a right to have his suspicion, but this wasn't the right time to address that suspicion. The other cats that worked for us didn't need to see that there may be some disagreement or dissension within the ranks. They needed to see that we were still strong and one team. That Reggie and Damian still had a bond and solid connection and no one could break that bond or come between them. I so wanted to scream through the phone and tell Damian to hand Reggie the damn phone. Unfortunately, he had pulled the phone away from his ear, so he couldn't hear me.

"Whatcha' trying to say Reggie?" I heard Damian ask. It sounded as if he had a lot of aggression in his voice and he was appalled at Reggic's allegation.

"Nigga, I said what I had to say loud and clear," I heard Reggie reply as if he wasn't backing down. "And everybody in this motherfucker heard me. So now you need to do some talking."

"Damian!" I yelled through the phone. But it became very apparent that he didn't hear me.

"Reggie, you know you wrong man. I don't know where the fuck this shit is coming from, but you know what you're saying ain't right and I don't appreciate you disrespecting me like that," Damian said in a moderate but sharp tone.

"Oh. so now you're feeling disrespected?" I heard my brother say in a sarcastic manner. Then he laughed. "Nigga, I'm the one getting disrespected here because I believe that your homeboy over there knows who robbed my motherfucking sister and killed one of my best men."

"Look, I can't speak for that man over there, but I do know that I had nothing to do with that shit that happened earlier. And for you to insinuate that I would put Naomi in harm's way isn't cool. You know I ain't that type of nigga Reggie. Damn, you and I have been boys all our fucking lives and Lil Sis has been like a sister to me."

Before Reggie could respond someone began to knock on the door at the apartment they were in. "Who is it?" I heard Reggie roar. But I couldn't hear the person's voice behind the door. I was having major difficulty hearing, so I waited to see what was about to happen next. And then three seconds later, I heard a man say, "Hey the police is back out here."

"How many is it?" Reggie asked.

"Just two," I heard the guy say.

"Where they at?" Reggie responded.

"They on foot and they walking around outside harassing some of them young boys who live in the other towers. Wait, hold on," the guy said and then the phone fell silent. "Gee just said they followed that nigga, Tony, into the second tower."

"A'ight, let's move before they come back out," I heard Reggie say. Then Damian's phone went dead. I didn't get a hello, goodbye or nothing. So I immediately pressed the send button again, but his voicemail came on after the first ring.

"Shit!" I spat and pressed the end button. Then I pressed the send again. And once again his fucking voicemail came on.

Frustrated beyond words, I tried my luck and decided to call my brother back. The phone rang three times before he finally answered. I found myself sighing all over again. "Reggie, what the fuck is going on?" I screamed through the phone. I wasn't happy by his performance in front of all those lame ass niggas he had working for us. It wasn't a good look for our operation. It didn't show cohesiveness. We were their leaders, Damian included, and you never allowed the peons to see any weakness amongst those in management. It was Business 101. The business venue didn't matter—it could be a ten million dollar car company or a ten million dollar drug, for the most part the same business principles applied. Only, when we got fucked, people died. That was our termination plan.

"Look, Naomi, I can't talk right now. I'm trying to get out of this building before we get spotted," he said to me. I could tell by the acoustics that he was in the stairwell trying to get down to the first floor.

"Reggie, we need to talk," I said immediately before he hung up on me. "I heard everything you said to

Damian and that was some foul shit and not a good look, especially in front of those guys out there."

"Look, I got everything under control," he told me and then he hung up on me. I knew his ass would do that. I was glad I got in what I did before he hung up. Hopefully it made his ass think before overreacting.

But I was still left speechless and helpless. What was really frustrating was that I couldn't do shit about it. Reggie said what he had to say to Damian. Damian said what he had to say back and I couldn't get a word in otherwise. That's not how I liked for things to be. I hated it when I couldn't control a situation. I was bothered to the tenth power and I couldn't say or do anything to prevent this shit from happening tonight. Whatever this shit was? I just hoped this whole thing would blow over before Reggie got any worse. Hell, we had just flown in a prime shipment of coke imported from South America, and we needed everyone on deck to get rid of this shit, so we can go back and re-up.

Being in the dope game didn't promise you a lifelong career of prosperity. In this type of business, you only had a couple of years to get a good run and save up as much money as you possibly could and get the fuck out. If you messed around and let someone come between that or get sidetracked, then you were the damn fool for overstaying your welcome. In other words, you deserved everything that fell on you for being stupid and greedy. At the end of the day, you were in charge of your own destiny. It was a simple motto, "get what you can while you can."

After I finally dozed off to sleep, my fucking Blackberry rang and woke me from a semi-sound sleep. When I heard Damian's voice, I calmed down a little. I peeped at my alarm clock and noticed that it was one-fifteen a.m. "Is everything all right?" I didn't hesitate to ask.

"Yeah, everything is cool," he answered. "I'm on my way to the Bronx to pick up some money this nigga owes me and then I'm gonna head to the crib."

"Where is Reggie?"

"When I left him he was still at the other spot."

"Did you guys get that shit straighten out?"

"Not really. Right after he smacked Walt upside the head with his pistol a couple times, he screamed on him and threatened to kill him if he didn't tell him who ran up on y'all today."

"What did Walt say?" I asked curiously.

"He denied having any involvement at all."

"What do you think? I mean, you know him better than any of us."

"I believed him. That's why I told Reggie to chill out and go at this thing another way. But you know how crazy he gets when we go against him, which is why I believed he started screaming on me."

"Did he say anything else to you after y'all left the spot?"

"Nah, he was quiet the whole drive until Vanessa called him."

"Well, did he say something to you when y'all finally parted ways?"

"He just told me to meet him back at the hideaway spot when I get up in the morning."

"You going?"

"Yeah, I'm going, what kinda question is that?"

I played off Damian's smartass remark. But he was right, that was a crazy ass question. If he didn't show, Reggie would hunt his ass down. "Are you going to talk to him about how he screamed on you in front of Dre and them?"

"Of course I am. I can't have that shit lingering out there and not do anything about it."

"Well, just make sure you handle the situation with kid gloves. You know how Reggie is when you question him about how he handles his business affairs. Not only that, we're family at the end of the day, so we gotta stick together. We've got too much shit going on right now to be falling apart at the seams behind some bullshit. Now I know we lost one of our soldiers and almost ten stacks, but we've still got to move on."

"You're right," Damian agreed. I could tell he was still pissed but I was glad he called. I could tell he was in better spirits. I just hoped Reggie was in even better spirits by the time they met several hours from now.

"I know I'm right," I stated. "So make things right with Reggie and call me tomorrow."

"A'ight," he said.

Chapter 6

Operation Get Money

I wasn't ready when my alarm clock went off at four in the morning. I had to literally drag myself out of bed and into the shower. By five, I was out the house and on the road, heading towards LaGuardia Airport. Thank God the traffic wasn't bad. I didn't live far from the airport and on early days like this it usually didn't take me long to get to work. But on days when I had a mid or late morning flight, the traffic would be backed up as soon as I hit the road.

I parked the truck and made my way inside the terminal. Every morning around this time I always saw the same fucking faces. A few worked for me and Reggie, but the rest of the lames were regular Joe Blows who worked their asses off for a fucking measly fifteen dollars an hour and they thought they were on top of the world. A couple of the bitches worked for the same airline as me and I considered them a part of the same Joe Blow -clique as the others. But these two troublemakers were in a class of their own. They were ass kissers who snitched on other flight attendants for the sake of brownie points.

One of the chicks was Suzie Malone and the other bitch was Rhonda Ashford. They both were flight attendants but they worked on different jetliners. I had worked with them occasionally and they weren't pleasant to work with, which was why I was very upset to find out that we were working the same flight this morning. Thankfully, my girl, Sabrina, was on the schedule with me, because I would have flipped out if I had to work with these bitches by myself.

Once our plane was airborne, Sabrina and I volunteered to serve refreshments to the passengers at the back of the plane, while Suzie and Rhonda worked the first class. Under normal circumstances, first class was Sabrina and my territory but we allowed them to handle it today, since there weren't any rich prospects for the taking.

During the course of the flight, Sabrina and I got a few stares and a couple of snide remarks but we kept it professional and ignored those hoes. Sabrina wasn't aware of my dealings and how important this job was for me, so I found myself having to remind her that those bitches weren't worth getting written up over. I also reminded her about the recession the country was presently in—so if she allowed them bitches to get her kicked out of a job, then she would be just another unemployed bitch standing in the dreaded unemployment line. It took awhile for her ass to get it, but after my five-minute pep talk, she saw the light and got the hint. America was fucked right now and another bitch in the soup line didn't bother the politicians or the wealthy swimming in dough.

"What would you like to drink ma'am?" I asked the first woman in the last row of the plane.

"Pretzels?" I heard Sabrina ask the woman on the opposite row. She and I handed out drinks and bags of pretzels to passengers in our section. And right before it was time to land our plane, she and I had to go back around to retrieve all of the trash that the passengers had to discard. When that was done, we took our seats and waited for our plane to land.

The landing was bumpy as usual but we landed safely. After all the passengers had exited the plane, it was the flight attendants' job to cross check to make sure no one left any of their belongings behind. So as Sabrina and I searched each row, we saw Suzie and Rhonda coming towards us. I stood up and faced them.

"We're going to need you two to rearrange the beverage cart y'all used because it's in disarray. And Rhonda and I aren't trying to get written up behind you guys laziness," Suzie said. I really wasn't in the mood for this petty shit today. But it is what it is when you get too many women working together. And that was the nature of the airline industry. Women working together and causing all kinds of unnecessary drama just for the sake of drama was a part of the course.

Before I went in on Suzie, I took one good look at this fucking blonde hair bimbo. She tried her best to look like Pamela Anderson, but she was way off with her fake fucking boobs and long blonde extensions. If she knew what was good for her, she'd better get the hell out of my damn face before Rhonda was picking her ass up off the floor.

I shook my head and gave that stank bitch the nastiest expression I could muster up. "First of all, what makes you think you can come back here and approach me Suzie?" I questioned her silly ass. "I don't fuck with you like that. And for you to tell me that Sabrina and I have to rearrange the beverage cart is really taking it to another level. Girl, if you don't get out of my damn face, I'm gonna say something that you really ain't gonna want to hear."

Sabrina chuckled, while I stood there and waited for Suzie's white ass to say something else stupid. Instead of making another comment, she rolled her eyes while her sidekick, Rhonda, said, "I told you she was going to act ghetto with you."

Appalled at this bitch's remark, I damn near spit out fire. "Ghetto!" I snapped as I placed my right hand across my hip. "Oh, you ass kissing bitches ain't seen ghetto." I snarled as I took one step towards them both.

"Come on, Suzie. Let's get out of here before she shows us how ghetto she can get," Rhonda advised Suzie as she grabbed her arm and pulled her back towards the front of the plane.

"Yeah, Suzie, you better listen to your dumbass friend, because she ain't gonna jump in to help you once I start whipping on your ass."

Sabrina laughed louder. And I started laughing too as I watched those two dizzy ass chicks run for cover.

"I'm not worried about you Naomi," Suzie responded. "I can take care of myself. And besides, it won't be long before I get your ass booted off this airline for all the underhanded stuff you're doing. Believe me, I got my eyes on you, sweetie."

"You better. Because I got my eyes on you too, you tramp," I roared. Thank God the pilots had already left the plane or I would've been in trouble for that outburst. I hope Suzie was talking about the small minor shit I was doing like being a pain in her ass, and not the real scandalous shit I was doing.

Sabrina tapped me on my shoulder. "You think she knows about you getting involved with some of the airline's male passengers?"

I turned around to give Sabrina my complete attention. I wanted her to see exactly how sincere I was about my response to her question. "Look, I could care less if she knew I fucked every man that walked onto this plane. What I do with those niggas is my business. But if I dare find out that she's going behind my back to talk to personnel about me, I am going to make that bitch very sorry that she ever met me."

"Damn, you're serious, huh?" Sabrina surmised.

"You damn right I am," I replied quickly. "Because I don't fuck with her, or anyone else for that matter. So she needs to stay the fuck out of my way before she gets hurt."

After I expressed to Sabrina what would happen to Suzie if she dared to open her mouth about me to my bosses, we finished what we were doing. Then we exited the plane. Our next flight wasn't for another two hours and Sabrina suggested we get some breakfast from the food court inside the New Orleans Airport terminal. While we waited for our food, she excused herself to call the guy she had just started seeing. She wanted to let him know that our flight made it safely to New Orleans. While she was preoccupied, I decided to call Reggie. I had to know if he and Damian had a chance to talk and bury the hatchet. But as fate would have it, his voicemail picked up after the first ring, so I assumed he had turned his phone off. Instead of calling Damian, I stuck my Blackberry back into my handbag and thought about how I would approach this situation when I did get him on the phone.

Reggie was my brother and I loved him to death. I knew his shortcomings and being paranoid was his biggest weakness. He was a man who had built a small but lucrative empire, and his life of hustling was coming back to haunt him.

Reggie was an innovator. He truly was a student of the game. He had taken the lessons of Al Capote, Frank Lucas, Nicky Barnes and many other gangsters, and used those lessons to forge his legacy. His product wasn't local, it was transported from South America via different locations to the states. I was his mule via my different flights throughout the United States. There were four cities I flew to often that were great points of entry to the U.S.: San Diego, Phoenix, Miami and Houston. These were also sites that the DEA patrolled and staked out regularly, but having connections with TSA bag handlers and customs officials kept us in business and more importantly, kept us stealth. And in this business, you had to fly under the radar.

During a recession, any extra dollar could help and Reggie fed on that fact. The money he paid our U.S. connections was worth it. And who couldn't use an extra ten grand during these trying times. Additionally, the take from the suppliers in South America was also lucrative.

So everyone was getting paid, including me.

And since Reggie wasn't dealing with a local supplier, he wasn't on the DEA's radar nor NYPD's Narcotics Division. NYPD didn't look at Reggie as being the big time dealer he was. They thought he was a third or fourth tier dealer, and that was fine by my brother. The less they thought of him, the more income he could bring in.

Maybe it helped that Reggie and I were both diversified financially. His best lesson was never keep your money in one place. As much as black people didn't believe in banks, those in the criminal element believed even less. *Reggie was different.* He had created at least five aliases for both of us, and we had bank accounts spread throughout the U.S. and an account in Switzerland and the Cayman Islands for both of us. My regular airline check was direct deposited into a local bank in New York. Reggie also owned a computer repair shop that had legitimate employees in the front of the shop, while a hidden staircase led to a basement where Reggie stashed drugs, weapons and money.

Lastly, because of his paranoia, Reggie believed in confiding in three people: me, Damian and our father, Miguel Foxx. If any one of us ever broke that trust, I believed Reggie would freak the fuck out. And there's no telling what he would do to get the revenge he thought he deserved. I just hoped that day would never come, because we all needed each other to maneuver around this cutthroat ass world. We had to keep this shit tight or all of us would be going down.

I was happy when my workday had ended and I was back in the city. As soon as I reached my car, Reggie called me. "What's up papi?" I asked him in a cheerful way.

"When did you get back in town?" he asked.

"My flight just landed about thirty minutes ago. Why?"

"I need you to come by my house and get this box for me," he said.

"Is Vanessa there?" I wanted to know.

"Nah, she ain't here yet. That's why I want you to hurry up," he said with urgency.

"Okay. I'll be there in about twenty minutes," I told him and then we disconnected our call.

During my drive to Reggie's place, I got a call from Marco. It was somewhat of a surprise to me because he told me he would be down in South America until the end of the week.

"Hello there," I said.

"How are you?" he asked in his very thick Hispanic accent.

"I'm doing great."

"Very good," he replied. "How is business?"

"Business is great. Everybody including Reggie is very happy."

"Very good. So, are you in the city?"

"Yes, I'm here. Why do you ask?"

"Because I'm leaving South America tomorrow to come back to New York for a few days and I want to see you."

"What time can I expect you?"

"Don't worry, I'll call you when I get there," he replied quickly.

"Okay. Great. I'll be waiting on your call," I assured him.

Before we ended our call, he told me how he'd missed me and that he wanted to bend me over and fuck the hell out of me. It had been a while since I had fucked Marco. Truthfully, I wasn't looking forward to it. His dick was no bigger than my thumb and after fucking him, I had to fuck somebody else just to get satisfied. Marco was the only reason I went out and bought me a battery-operated boyfriend. I understood why women had them a BOB; because of non-fucking or unendorsed motherfuckers like Marco. To be candid, the only reason I fucked him in the beginning was because Reggie and I needed him to supply us. He was our South America connection and on top of that, he had the pure shit. His shit rocked. I didn't use drugs, but when we made the connection with Marco and our shit hit the streets, Reggie's fame immediately shot through the roof. He was the toast of the city for supplying some fire shit. That was why we were surprised he wasn't on anyone's radar like DEA or NYPD.

On that level, Marco was the man with the best shit and top of that he was a fucking millionaire at best and I loved the perks that came with being his flavor of the month. Marco's money could be used as wrapping paper to wrap around this entire fucking globe. He was a well-known cocaine supplier and executioner. He was someone you didn't fuck with. I was turned on by his money and status, not his dick. And now that I had my own money and was able to buy myself a $30,000 Hermes Birkin bag or $110,000 Maserati Spyder, I honestly had no use for the old man. I'd let him eat my pussy if he'd like. But that was as far as I was going to let it go.

At the end of our conversation, he told me to tell Reggie to be available before he left town, because he needed to have a meeting with him. I assured him I'd do just that.

CHAPTER 7

The Penthouse Suite

Reggie wasn't too happy with me because I let Vanessa beat me to their apartment. She let me inside of their fifteenth floor penthouse suite. She kept herself laced in five hundred dollar blouses and six hundred dollar skirts and slacks made from Gucci, Valentino and Marc Jacobs. Her shoe game was more fierce than her wardrobe. When I looked at her Valentino sunny check dress, I knew she'd hit my brother up for at least five grand and been shopping recently, because this dress just came in this season. It was no secret that she was a label whore and was consistently in competition with me, but whether she knew it or not, I wasn't fazed by her antics. I was the queen around here so everything she did to make herself feel like she was better than me was done in vain. As usual, I acted like I was happy to see her.

"What's up mommy?" I greeted her by extending a hug.

"I'm good. What's up with you?" she replied as she hugged me back. She gave me this whack ass pat on my back as she embraced me. I could tell she didn't want to hug me. But I left well enough alone because she was being her normal self. And as long as she wanted to play her games, I vowed to do the same thing.

"You know me. I'm always on the hunt to find ways to get rich so I can retire from my daytime gig."

"Just follow your brother's lead and you'll be just fine," she assured me and then she closed the front door behind us.

"Where is he anyway?" I asked her as I started walking down the hallway towards their family room.

"He's in the back watching TV," she told me.

I continued down the hallway and then I entered into the family room where I found Reggie slipping on his Prada flip flops. "Where are you going?" I asked him.

He took his wallet off the coffee table and said, "Come on, let's take a ride to see mom and dad."

I was not in the mood to drive out to the Bronx to see our parents. They relocated to White Plains a couple years ago from Harlem. My mom thought the move would do our father some good. When you hear people say, "You can take the person out the ghetto, but you can't take the ghetto out the person," believe them." That was exactly what my mom was going through with our father. He loved the fucking streets.

"What's over there?" I whined. I was tired physically as well as mentally, so I wasn't in any way feeling this trip.

"I wanna drop some dough off to moms. And see how they're doing. She said she hasn't seen you in a couple of weeks, that's why I got you to come over here and go along with me."

I sighed. "I wished you would've told me this over the phone."

"If I would've, you would not have come," he replied and then he reached back down on the sofa and retrieved his pistol from behind one of the decorative pillows.

"What are you about to do with that?" I asked him.

"I'm taking it with me," he told me and then he stuck it down in the waist of his shorts. Once he covered it with his shirt, he was ready to step out of the house.

"I thought you were staying in the house tonight?" Vanessa asked immediately after she entered the room. She stood at the entryway and waited for Reggie's reply. I stood there alongside Reggie and waited to see how he was going to handle this situation.

"Look Vanessa, I ain't got time for this shit tonight," he replied.

"You ain't never got time for my shit! But I know what you're doing," she spat as she continued to stand in the entryway of the living room. "I'm not stupid, I know you got Naomi to come over and get you like y'all are going to go and handle some business. But you gon' get her to drop your no-good ass off over one of your bitches houses!"

I stood there looking shocked. I had no idea what the hell she was talking about. If Reggie wanted me to drop him off at one of his hoes house, he hadn't said anything to me about it. "Please don't put me in y'all mess today," I begged.

"It's too late, because you're already in it," she replied sarcastically.

"Oh, no, it's not too late, because I am out of here," I told her and then I made my way out of the living room area. I headed back down the hallway towards the front door. Reggie wasn't too far behind me.

"You don't know what the fuck you're talking about. Now get out of my face with that dumb shit," I heard him say as he stormed passed her.

Vanessa didn't let him get too far. She was hot on his trail. "Don't you walk away from me Reggie. I am so tired of you disrespecting me with all your bitches and staying out all times of the night!" she yelled as she stormed behind him. And when she got within arm's reach of him, she grabbed him by the back of his shirt and tried to prevent him from leaving. I stood by the front door and watched as the drama unfolded.

Reggie turned around abruptly and pushed Vanessa away from him. I watched as she stumbled backwards. "Keep your fucking hands off me and take your ass back out there in the street and go be with that nigga you was laid up with all day," he snapped.

I could see the embarrassment on her face. I wanted to say something, but I kept my comment and opinion to myself. This wasn't the first time I witnessed them fighting. This drama had been going on for years.

"Did you see him just hit me?" she belted out. But I turned my back to her and opened up the front door. "You ain't gotta answer me. But don't be trying to talk to me later when I call the police on his ass and get him arrested for putting his fucking hands on me."

"Let's go," Reggie instructed me as he pushed me out into the hallway.

Immediately after he closed the front door behind us, Vanessa had the audacity to open up the front door and come out in the hallway behind us. But Reggie coaxed me to continue towards the elevator. That didn't stop Vanessa from continuing on with her rampage. "Fuck both of you motherfuckers! Don't come calling me when y'all need somebody to bail y'all asses out of jail!" she screamed behind us.

"I'm not doing shit wrong to go to jail!" I yelled back and then Reggie and I hopped on the elevator.

After the doors closed, I exhaled. "How the fuck you deal with her? She is wreck-less as hell! I mean, who comes out into the hallway of a building you live and insinuates that your man and his sister dabble in illegal activity?"

"She does."

"Well, you need to nip that shit in the bud before she gets you locked up for some far more serious shit then whipping her ass!"

"Don't worry. As soon as I get my paper up the way I want, I'm gonna dip out on her dumbass."

"Really?"

"You damn right. And I'm looking forward to that day too."

"Wait, so you think she's fucking around on you?"

"Nah, I don't think that."

"So, why did you say that back in the house?"

"Come on now Naomi, you slipping," Reggie said and smiled. "Niggas blame shit they do on their women all the time. That way, we can take the heat off us."

"So wait, am I really dropping you off to one of your bitches cribs?"

"Nah, we gon' go and see moms and pops," Reggie replied and then we hopped off the elevator.

During the drive to the Bronx, I tried to touch on the subject about him and Damian. But he didn't bite. I could tell he wasn't in the mood to discuss anything dealing with what happened last night. He did, however, tell me that he and Damian were going to link up and handle some business later. So I left well enough alone. I figured they must've come to some mutual understanding and moved on.

My parents' house sat on the corner of Gun Hill and White Plains Road. It wasn't the newest or the most posh house in the world, but it was better than where we grew up in the Polo Grounds. Even though they changed addresses, my pops kept that same street mentality.

I wished I could say Carter Foxx was a retired hustler, but I couldn't. Our dad was a forever man of the streets. He was semi-retired at best. He still hit the streets every now and then. *To keep my skills up,* he would tell us.

Reggie and our dad were close. He taught Reggie at a young age all of the rules of the game. If Reggie had an issue, especially dealing with business, he bounced it off Carter Foxx.

As always, when we showed up, my mom would sit us down and practically shove food down our throats. It was her Hispanic culture to always cook and have family over. That's how we found time to bond with one another. So we chatted a bit and caught up.

After the four of us had dinner, Mom excused herself because she knew we needed to talk business.

She didn't know my part in Reggie's business but she suspected I was doing way more than the lies I told her. She always warned me that I was doing well in a legitimate job and I shouldn't mess that up.

Foxx listened intensely as Reggie ran down everything that had occurred. We called our dad by our last name—Foxx. I couldn't remember referring to him as dad. He taught us what he could, and that meant we knew the streets. I loved the man. He was a loving and caring like a father should be, but cool and down with knowledge, usable knowledge—the kind of teaching that kept you alive from one day to the next.

He was a slim man, slightly standing over five feet seven, a couple of inches shorter than my mom and Reggie, and an inch taller than me. His hair was naturally wavy with streaks of gray in his black locks, lending credence to his wisdom.

"I ever tell you about the time I recommended a runner for Stone business?" Foxx asked us after Reggie had went in-depth about the events that took place at the Polo Grounds yesterday. We both shook our heads no. Stone was Big Joey Stone, an enforcer and some say assassin, who was Foxx's best friend. "Well, I gave this guy, Marlo, who I was locked up with in the joint, my recommendation to work for Stone. A couple of weeks later, the motherfucker ran off with Stone's money and dope."

As kids we grew up on Foxx's stories, or misadventures, as our mom used to describe them. But somehow they had a therapeutic value to them, probably more so for Reggie. At the end of each story, was a lesson and today that was what my brother was looking for—the lesson in all of this madness.

"Well, we are talking about Stone here and the man knew everybody and everything. It took him a day to track Marlo down in the Bronx, and the house he was hiding in, they were waiting on Stone. It was a good old fashioned ambush. Well, Stone being Stone, he sniffed it out and handled his business. Six people died that day including Marlo.

"Of course, everyone thought I would be the seventh, but I met Stone at his house and apologized for recommending Marlo. I told him I didn't know the deal, and after he threw some bullshit questions at me, all was copacetic. I was Stone's best friend. The man knew I wouldn't betray him for nothing in the wrong. That's the value of friendship."

We were silent for a good minute. I think we both had to take in what Foxx had just relayed to us. I knew Reggie was searching for the message in the music. "So you saying Damian would not sell me out and this Walt nigga probably done this shit on his own or was a plant by somebody like Sheffield," Reggie stated.

"Exactly what I'm saying about Damian and about this cat Walt, but Sheffield is not your man. Sheffield is happy making dough slinging dope and pimping sluts throughout New York and New Jersey to want your action."

Sheffield was probably the oldest gangster in the New York area. Hell, he was the man when Foxx and Big Joey Stone were younger. The legend as told to us by Foxx was that Sheffield was really the front man for Stone's operation, but no one knew it. When Stone really wanted out of the business, he turned the business completely over to Sheffield. From that day forth, Sheffield provided Stone with ten percent of the profits on the first of every month like clockwork.

"Then who?" Reggie asked.

"Son, you are at the top of the food chain now. You have graduated to the top spot on the radar. The DEA and Narcotics Division may not know about you yet, but they will soon find out. Your success has painted this target on your back. So you better be very careful because someone is going to try to take you down a couple of notches or try to get you eliminated altogether."

Once again, silence filled the room. I could see the wheels grinding and turning in Reggie's head. Additionally, Foxx was his usual calm self. I was the deer in the headlights.

Carter Foxx broke the silence. "Let me ask around and see if I can find out if somebody knows who set y'all up and killed your boy. I can almost guarantee that if it was somebody from uptown, then some of my people will know who did it."

My dad never ceased to amaze me. He and Stone knew everyone, and who they didn't know, someone in their circle knew that person. I smiled inside at Reggie's strategy to come talk to the master. After all, most of what he knew he learned from Foxx.

"I think you did right kicking his ass and putting him on notice," Foxx continued. "If he is the spy and played the part well, he will stick around and see if he can get some info on you for his boss. Assuming he is working for someone else. But be careful and chill 'til I get back with you. Now what's this Walt last name?"

"Granger," Reggie replied. "Walt Granger. He's supposed to be related to that nigga Gerald Granger that caught that murder rap a couple years ago for setting them niggas on fire from the Pink Houses."

"Oh, okay," my dad said as if he'd remember exactly whom Reggie was talking about.

We chilled a little, talking about other things. Foxx filled us in on the necessity of being vigilant and respecting the game. He didn't want us getting too high strung on the game, and reiterated to Reggie on watching his back. As he stated, "Top dog always have the biggest bull's eye on his back."

That was the Foxx we loved. The man who lived by the streets, and unfortunately, one day would probably die by the streets. But he was a man who would do anything for his kids. If he said he would get the lowdown on Walt, he would; even if it meant turning over every damn rock in the five boroughs of New York.

CHAPTER 8

Unnecessary Drama

While Reggie and I were visiting our parents, Vanessa was blowing his fucking phone up. She called every bit of thirteen times back to back. And Reggie did not answer one call. He eventually turned off his phone so we could continue our talk with our dad in peace.

On the way out, Reggie and I kissed our mom, and Foxx walked us both out to my truck. I handed Reggie my car keys and climbed into the passenger seat. My dad closed the door behind me and then he leaned up against the passenger side door. "How is everything at home?" he looked directly at Reggie and asked.

"It's hell!" I blurted out. "Vanessa is taking him through the ringer. And she's been provoking him lately so he can put his hands on her, so she can get him locked up."

"It's gotten that bad?" my dad asked.

"Worse!" Reggie commented.

"Well, whatever you do. Don't put your hands on that girl. You got too much shit riding on you to fuck it up behind her."

"I tell him that all the time," I chimed in.

"I hope he's listening to you then. Because ain't nothing worse than going to jail because you done whipped your woman's ass," my dad commented and then he chuckled. "It ain't worth it."

"I got everything under control," Reggie assured him and then he turned on the ignition.

My dad kissed me on the cheek and stepped away from the passenger side door. "I'ma hold you to that," he said. "Now y'all take care."

"A'ight," Reggie said.

"Love you," I blurted out as Reggie drove off.

Reggie wasted no time getting us back on the Cross Bronx Expressway. It was late in the evening and I was dead tired, so when he asked me if he'd be able to borrow my truck, I happily obliged. But before he dropped me off I managed to tell him that Marco would be in town tomorrow.

"I thought he was going to be in South America until next week," Reggie stated.

"I thought so too," I replied. "But he called and said he'll be in town tomorrow. He also told me to tell you to be available, because he wants to have a meeting with you before he leaves."

"Did he say how long he was going to be in town?"

"I think he said a day or two. Either way, he won't be here long so please answer your Blackberry when I call you," I instructed him. "So where are you on your way to tonight?"

"Since Vanessa thinks that I'm going over to one of my bitches house, that's where I'm going."

I was never shocked by Reggie's candor, but he took it to another level with this remark. I backhanded him in his left arm. "You are terrible! You suppose to be the bigger person and prove to your wife that she's wrong and that you don't cheat. Maybe then, she'll act like she's got some damn sense. I told you a long time ago that a happy wife will give you a happy life. As long as Vanessa is happy and knows that you're respecting her and you're not out here fucking around on her with your mistresses, then everything at home would be peaceful and cozy."

Reggie sucked his teeth. "That shit doesn't work. Remember we're talking about Vanessa. That bitch is never satisfied with anything I give her. It seems like the more I give her greedy ass, the more she wants. You should see all the fucking receipts she's got from Neiman and Saks. She's probably got more fucking Giuseppe Zanottis and Christian Louboutins than you."

I burst into laughter. "Correction. No one in the city has more Zanottis and Red Bottoms than me. Remember Marco nicknamed me *New York's Finest.* So I dress the part. And don't you ever forget that," I replied sarcastically and then I smacked him against his arm again.

We both laughed because Reggie knew I loved expensive handbags, shoes and clothes, and for that reason alone I didn't fuck with cats that didn't drop at least ten grand on a shopping trip for me. Since I was now making my own dough with our business venture, I didn't need a man to do shit for me. However, if they're trying to take me out with plans to eventually get me into bed, then they would have to pay dearly.

After Reggie dropped me off, I went inside of my apartment and took a long, hot shower. When I got out the shower I noticed my phone was beeping, which indicated someone had called and left me a message. I picked up my phone and realized that Damian had tried to call me twice, so I dialed his number back and put the call on speakerphone, that way my hands could be free to dry myself off.

"What's good?" he answered.

"Nothing much. Returning your call."

"Yeah, I called you twice."

"I'm sorry. But I was in the shower."

"Why didn't you invite me over so I could wash your back?" he said and then he chuckled. But I knew he was serious.

"You know I'm not messing with you like that."

"Why not? You let those old niggas get at you."

"That's because they pay like they weigh," I chuckled.

"My paper may not be as long as that nigga, Marco, or any of those other cats you fucked with, but I can pay like I weigh too."

"Come on now, Damian, you already know what time it is. We can't fuck around like that, we're like brother and sister."

"I ain't never said that shit."

I chuckled once again. "No, you haven't but you know it'll be weird as hell going out with you."

"I don't know why you be throwing me to the sharks. I keep telling you to stop messing with those old ass men before you get the worms, and start fucking with me because I can take better care of you."

After I finished drying off with the towel, I sat down on my bed and began to rub lotion all over my body. Meanwhile, Damian continued to express his feelings towards me. And what was so bizarre about the whole thing was that I was really enjoying it. He turned me on as I listened to him explain how he'd take care of me. And at one point while he was talking, I pictured him thrusting my legs open while I was naked and sucking the hell out of my pussy. I heard from a few chicks around the way that he gave some good head.

"Damian, you know I got my chips stacked up pretty high, so I don't need a man to take care of me. You could come 'round here and give me some head though," I mentioned and then I laughed. I said it in a jokingly way, but I was serious as a heart attack.

"I'm on my way now," he replied.

"Wait!" I screamed through the phone. "I was just playing. So you better not bring your butt over here."

"You better stop playing with me. You know I've been crazy about you for a long time now. And I would've married you a long time ago if you'd given me a chance."

"Damian, let's not dwell on the past. We're doing big things now so let's focus on that," I encouraged him.

"Yeah, a'ight. But one day, I'll get you to change your mind," he insisted.

I smiled. "I'm sure you will," I mumbled. "So I hear you and Reggie are going to meet up tomorrow to handle some business," I changed the subject.

"Yeah, we gotta make a couple runs."

"So I take it you two are okay now?" I probed.

"You know your brother ain't the type of nigga that's gonna apologize for the fucked up shit he does, so I'm not even sweating it. I let that shit go right after it happened."

He was right about Reggie. Besides saying "I'm sorry" to me or our parents, the words didn't exist in his vocabulary for anyone else. "Well, do what works for you. So have you heard anything?"

"Nah, not yet. But I gotta couple of people on it. Don't worry, somebody's gonna slip up and say something."

"I know."

Damian let out a long sigh. "Well, since you ain't gon' invite me over, then I'ma holla at you tomorrow."

"Yeah, you do that," I told him. Immediately after I hung up with him, I sat back on my bed and imagined how he would be as my man. He was definitely my type. I loved a dark skinned man. Plus, he had the right height and a nice body. And to make his package complete, I knew he was sitting on a nice fat nest egg. He was my brother's right hand man, so I knew he was raking in the same amount of dough as I was and even more. On a weekly average, we were pushing about five kilos of coke, which meant we were making at least $800k per week.

What a lot of people didn't know was that we got our coke raw and uncut. So we were able to step on it three times and that made us be able to triple our quantity, without damaging the quality. To the average user or someone coked out of their mind, it still felt like it was pure. It was easy math and we learned very quickly. And the most promising part about it all was that I was able to get our product through the airport customs without any hassles.

Of course, I had my team of TSA agents working around the clock making sure my shit got through. We all knew if it weren't for the shipping program that our airline had in place for major corporations who were in good standings, then we'd be up shit's creek.

This was how it worked: once or twice a month we'd get our shipments to come in under a well-known corporation's name that had been using our airlines to ship their goods for a long time. Since they paid top dollar for us to ship their goods, we, in turn, didn't x-ray or scan anything that came through our channels with their labels on it. And since me and my team knew this, we would get that company's registration code and shipping labels and place it on the containers that concealed Marco's coke so it could come through with ease. So far, we had been lucky. I was keeping my fingers cross that we could make a few more hits before our trail got hot.

CHAPTER 9

The Boss Man

We had the short run today from New York to Chicago and back. I was back in the city by six that evening. Marco was already in town and wanted me to come see him at once. I believed I had a ten-minute debate with him about me going home first so I could change. But he insisted that I come directly to his apartment on the Upper East Side of Manhattan. He assured me that he had something very cozy for me to change into. He should have known I wasn't going to listen to him. I liked having shit go my way. Instead of going by his place first, I stopped off at mine as I had planned. I instructed my valet to keep my truck outside because I was only running in my apartment for a few seconds.

While en route, my Blackberry rang. I couldn't answer it because I was in the elevator and I knew the call would drop. So I ignored it. I knew it wouldn't be important anyway because it was Vanessa. She either wanted to complain to me about how Reggie was still cheating on her or she wanted to warn me about how she planned to call the police if he hit her again. Unfortunately for me, her calls persisted. She called me four times straight, so on the fifth call I decided to answer it.

She started wailing through the phone as soon as she heard my voice. "Naomi, Reggie's in the hospital."

Alarmed by her outburst, I dropped my house keys on the floor directly in front of my front door. “What for? Is he all right?”

“He was shot,” she continued to sob uncontrollably.

I reached down and picked my keys up from the floor. “Which hospital is he in?” I panicked as I ran to the elevator.

“New York Presbyterian.”

“I’m on my way there now,” I assured her.

Immediately after I hung up with Vanessa, I got back onto the elevator and headed back down to my car. As soon as I got in the car, I dialed Damian’s number.

“Hello,” he answered with urgency.

“Hey, I just got a call from Vanessa saying Reggie’s been shot,” I replied still in panic mode as I made a quick right turn onto 8th Avenue from 49th Street.

“I know, I just talked to her too. I’m on my way to the hospital now,” hc stated.

“Alright. Well, I’ll meet you there,” I told him and then disconnected the call.

I couldn’t tell you if my truck had wings or not, but after I sped down West Side Highway, got off at Exit 17 and merged onto Riverside Drive, I was on Broadway in less than nine minutes flat. It took me forever to find a good parking space. After circling the block several times, I finally decided to park my truck in the hospital’s parking garage, since it was the weekend and valet service was not available.

When I entered into the emergency room area, my heart raced as I sprinted over to the information desk. There was this little Asian woman sitting behind the glass partition when I approached it.

"How can I help you?" she asked me.

"I just got a call that my brother, Reggie Foxx, was just brought in to the ER for a gunshot wound," I explained.

"Yes, he did," she replied immediately. "Have a seat in the waiting area and someone will be out to answer any questions you may have."

"Can you at least tell me where he was shot? Or how he's doing?" I pressed the issue.

"I'm sorry ma'am, but I'm not at liberty to say," she replied apologetically.

Frustrated by this woman's lack of compassion, I snapped and said, "You mean to tell me that you can't tell me where my brother was shot?"

"No. I'm sorry but I can't," she insisted.

Right before I was about to unleash my rage, I was grabbed from the back. And when I looked and realized that it was Damian, I calmed down. "Hey come over here and have a seat before she calls hospital security," he advised.

I followed him over to the seating area of the waiting room. "Have you seen Vanessa yet?" I asked as I took a seat in a chair next to the window.

"She's in the back answering some questions for the doctor."

"Did you find out what happened?"

"Not really. All she said was that some niggas shot him in front of this apartment building on 48th between Lexington and 3rd while he was trying to get into his car."

"Oh shit! That's Midtown-East. He was coming from Malika's apartment."

"Malika, with the Porshe truck?"

"Yeah," I answered.

"I thought he stopped fucking with her months ago. And when did she move over to that side of town?"

"When Reggie found out she was pregnant about six weeks ago. He put her up in that spot right before we got that shipment last week."

"Say word."

With tears falling down my face, I assured Damian that what I was saying was the absolute truth.

"Wow! So this nigga's got a baby on the way by Malika?" he pressed the issue as if he couldn't believe what his ears were hearing.

"That's what he told me," I replied nonchalantly.

"I thought they'd never get back together after all that shit that went down with Vanessa finding out about them. I remember Vanessa tried to kill Malika when she caught all of us coming out of Sylvia's Soulfood spot that night."

"Well, I don't think they're back together. He just said that he's gonna look out for her while she's carrying his baby," I continued. I honestly wasn't in the mood to discuss paternity issues and whether or not they were seeing each other again. What was near and dear to my heart was knowing Reggie's condition, whether or not he was going to be all right.

Thankfully, Vanessa came in the waiting room area a few minutes later. I jumped to my feet and met her in the middle of the floor. "Is he all right?" I wondered out loud.

Damian was down on my heels. "Yeah, is he alright?" he chimed in as well.

I could tell Vanessa had been crying a lot longer than I was because her eyes were blood shot red and visibly puffy. So when she opened her mouth, Damian and I both were waiting on pins and needles to hear what she had to say.

"He was shot in the left shoulder and his left leg. He lost a lot of blood, so the doctor operating on him said he may need a blood transfusion. Other than that, his injuries aren't life threatening so he should be fine after surgery."

I let out a sigh of relief. And without thinking about it, I grabbed Vanessa into my arms. She stood very stiff with her arms hanging by her side. And when I realized this, I let her go and stepped back from her. I wanted so badly to ask her what her damn problem was, but my mouth wouldn't open. Damian, of course, saw this and grabbed me by the arm.

"Come on. Let's go back and sit down," he instructed me.

I turned around to look at him and when I looked at his facial expression, I noticed how he wanted me to get away from Vanessa as quickly as possible. I didn't put up a fuss and followed him back to where we were sitting before this bitch walked in.

Vanessa took a seat on the other side of the waiting room. I watched her as she took her iPhone from her handbag and began texting someone. As time passed, the bitch continued to text her life away. She acted as if Damian and I weren't even in the same damn room. I shook my head and turned my focus towards Damian.

Meanwhile, my Blackberry rang. I looked down at the screen and noticed that it was Marco. I had forgotten that quickly that I was supposed to have met him at his apartment. I looked at Damian and sighed.

"What's wrong?" he asked.

"I was supposed to meet Marco before I got the call from Vanessa. And this is him calling me now."

"Are you going to tell him what happened?" he asked me with concern written all over his face.

"I'm not sure. What do you think? I mean we don't know why Reggie was shot. And you know Marco's gonna ask," I said and waited for Damian to give me the go ahead.

Before he could respond, my phone stopped ringing. So I held it in the palm of my hand and debated on whether or not to call him back.

"Nah, wait," Damian finally spoke up. "Don't tell him anything right now. Remember how paranoid he is and if he thinks we're having problems out here, then he's liable to shut our supply off and disappear from the face of this earth. So let's wait until Reggie comes out of surgery and sees what he says."

"Well, what excuse am I going to give him about why I didn't meet him when in fact I told him I would?" I asked curiously.

"I can't help you with that," Damian replied facetiously. "But you're a woman so I know you'll come up with something."

I cracked a smile. This was the first time I smiled since finding out Reggie had gotten shot. I knew Damian made this remark to simply make me smile. I poked him in his side. "Don't play with me. You know men are masters at the lying game."

"Nah, I doubt that," he chuckled as he looked back over at Vanessa who was still texting someone. "I wonder who the fuck she's texting," he changed the subject.

I looked at Vanessa with a disgusted look on my face. I figured that whoever she was texting had to be saying some pretty good stuff because she'd been going at it for close to forty minutes nonstop. I couldn't stand the sight of her so I turned my attention back to my phone. When I did that, I immediately thought to myself what was I going to tell Marco? I knew he'd be pissed off if I stood him up. I knew he would even be more furious to know that he'd tried to call me and I wouldn't answer his call nor call him back and explained my whereabouts. I sat there and wracked my brain trying to figure out what I was going to tell him. He was a man who always wanted answers no matter how bad it was. He detested liars and if he found out someone lied to him, he'd make their lives a living hell.

So what was I going to do?

Chapter 10

Changing the Rules

Damian and I sat in the waiting area of the ER for a total of five hours before we finally received word from the surgeon that Reggie was okay and didn't need a blood transfusion. The doctor said he was doing fine, a little weak from surgery, but he should easily rebound from the two shots he received.

I was so happy to hear the good news. My first question for the doctor was when Damian and I could see him?

"He's being transported to ICU right now," the doctor responded. "So give the nurses about thirty minutes or so and then you'd be able to go back and see him."

"That's good news," Damian spoke up.

"Yes it is," I agreed.

"Since he's on his way to the ICU, is there a certain number of visitors he can have at one time?" Vanessa asked out of the blue. I was taken aback by her question. I looked at her like she was fucking crazy. I mean, what kind of question was that? Was she trying to imply that she needed to be the only person going back there to see him? I swear I wanted to ask her exactly what she meant when she asked the doctor that question, but I decided against it. I knew now wasn't the time to chew her silly ass out. Not in front of the doctor anyway.

"Well, when we have patients in ICU, hospital policy only allows visits from family members," he explained.

Vanessa turned her attention from the doctor and looked directly at Damian. "I know you're his wife," the doctor stated to Vanessa. "Are you two related to him?" he asked Damian and I.

"Yes, we're both related. I'm his sister and this is his brother," I said and then I looked over at Vanessa and waited for the bitch to say anything that would suggest the opposite. I knew she was a loose cannon and she was prone to say anything. But she also knew my elevator didn't go all the way up to the top floor and that I would fuck her up when it came to Reggie. Trust me, she knew where to draw the line when it came to me.

"Okay then. Well, I guess you all would be fine," the doctor finally said. He gave us the impression that he sensed some tension. I could tell he was a bit uncomfortable standing there. Within seconds he excused himself, probably shaking his head at black people and their unnecessary drama.

Vanessa stormed back to the seat she had claimed. I stood in the same spot and shook my head with disgust. "She is so lucky that we're in a public place, because I would blast her ass right here on the spot!" I said, damn near on the verge of tearing the skin off my lips with my teeth.

Damian grabbed me by my arm and pulled me back to where we were sitting. "Come on. She's not even worth it," he commented.

I sat back down with Damian sitting next to me. He wrapped his arm around my shoulder to console me. I tried to relax and let her antics run off my back but I couldn't. "Look at her sitting there with that $75,000 iced out Presidential Rolex on her fucking wrist and flicking with those five carat VS1 diamond hoops in her ears. My brother risked his life out there in those fucking streets so he could buy all that shit for her ungrateful ass."

"I helped Reggie pick that joint out. And I got his jeweler to add the diamond bezel to it," Damian said in a reminiscent way.

"He told me. So to think that she has a problem with you or me going back to see Reggie is a slap in the face. I told him from day one that bitch wasn't shit. I swear I can't wait until he gets rid of her ass."

Damian continued to massage my back. A short while later, a nurse came in from ICU and notified us that we could go back and see Reggie. I was so happy to hear the news that I literally raced completely pass the nurse and into the ICU. "He's in room 119," I heard her say.

I think I counted like six rooms before I reached Reggie's room. When I pushed opened the door and saw him laid in the hospital bed with his eyes closed, while an I-V was attached to one arm and monitor devices were stuck to his chest, I almost wanted to cry my heart out. He looked so helpless in that bed. Knowing that I couldn't do a thing to make him feel better was devastating. My eyes started wailing up with tears, but I held them back. I knew I had to be strong for the both of us.

"Is he sleep?" Damian asked when he entered the room behind me.

Vanessa came into the room directly behind Damian. "Oh my baby!" she began to sob in a dramatic way and then she rushed over by his side. "Look at all this shit they got on him," she griped as she took inventory of his body.

I walked over and stood on the opposite side of the body with Damian standing by my side. "I wonder if he can hear us?" Damian asked out of curiosity.

"I'm sure he can," I chimed in.

Vanessa sucked her teeth and said, "Well, if he could don't you think he would've opened his eyes by now?"

I looked at her with the nastiest facial expression I could muster up. "Look, Vanessa, right now isn't the time to be getting flip at the lips. My brother is laid up in this bed and I'm sure he's going to be in a lot of pain when his drugs wear off, so can we leave the sarcasm and the bullshit at the door out of respect for him?"

"First of all, this is my motherfucking husband. And while he's incapable of making decisions, the hospital calls on me. So if anybody is going to get some respect around here, it's going to be me. Because at the end of the day, I got the last say so, not you. And if I wanted to be nasty, I could have both of y'all asses kicked out of here."

"Well, bitch, do it! I dare you ho!" I snapped. I couldn't hold back my rage any longer. I tried my best to get around to the other side of the bed but Damian wouldn't let me get by him.

"Let her go Damian. I ain't scared of her. Because as soon as she lay one finger on me, I am going to have her ass locked up on the spot," Vanessa threatened.

"Bitch, do you think I care about getting locked up? I would love to go to jail behind whipping your ass. See, I'm not afraid of you calling the police on me. I'm not my brother. I would kill your motherfucking ass and wouldn't think nothing of it!" I roared while Damian held onto me with all the strength in his body.

I take it some of the hospital staff heard us arguing because they came in within minutes of the drama beginning. The same female nurse who gave us Reggie's room number came into the room with two white male security guards in tow.

"I'm sorry but we're gonna have to ask you all to leave this room," she said.

"She's the one being volatile. Make her leave," Vanessa blurted out.

"Which one of you is the patient's wife?" the nurse asked as she looked at both me and Vanessa.

"I'm his wife so I shouldn't have to leave his side, especially when I'm not the one threatening bodily harm."

"Oh, bitch, stop being phony. You and I both know that my brother can't stand your ass for real. And if he was up right now, he'd tell them to tell your stinking ass to take a fucking hike instead of me."

"Stop lying to these people and get your ass out of here like they said," Vanessa replied sarcastically.

And then she laughed at me like this whole thing was a joke to her. I swear I lost it then.

"Oh, so this shit here is a game, huh? Well, since you're laughing bitch, know that I got a little niece or nephew on the way and it ain't by you. You trifling ass dog. Now laugh at that bitch!" I said and then I spit on the floor in her direction. I didn't give her a chance to come back at me with any more of her remarks because I exited the room immediately. And as I walked away I felt vindicated. It felt really good to give her a taste of her own medicine even though it was at the expense of Reggie. I just hoped he wouldn't be too upset with me when he woke up and found out that I let the cat out of the bag. Oh well, what's done was done. And I guess I would have to deal with it when the subject came back up.

Outside of the hospital, Damian walked me to my truck. Before we departed ways, he told me it would be best to tell Marco where Reggie was. But it would also be best to make Marco think that Reggie was at the wrong place at the wrong time and that the bullets were for someone else who lived in that neighborhood. This way Marco wouldn't think that Reggie was a potential target of a rival dealer and that our organization was solid. Leaving Marco with no worries was the plan.

I had to dig deep and come up with a clever but plausible story. I used the drive back to my apartment to come up with a good storyline. And after I put everything down and settled down, I picked up my phone and called him. He didn't sound very happy, but after I told him where I had been and who I had been there to see, he told me not to say any more and that he would send a car to come get me at once.

"You still want me to come over? Hell, it's almost one in the morning," I asked, hoping he'd hear how tired I was and tell me he'd see me later today. But my words went through one ear and out the other.

"Yes, it's very important that you come here to see me tonight because I plan on flying out of here later today."

I let out a long sigh. "Alright. Well, I guess I'll see you in a few."

CHAPTER 11

Marco's Empire

Marco's driver arrived at my apartment building in less than thirty minutes. And it took him less time to get me back to Marco's penthouse suite located on the Upper West Side. As soon I entered into his quarters I found him lounging on his hand made Italian leather recliner, smoking a Cuban cigar. I was surprised to see that he wasn't alone. He had another gentleman sitting on his hand made Italian leather sofa directly across from him. The gentleman stood to his feet and extended his hand as I approached them. "Naomi, I'd like to introduce you to my son, Miguel."

"Nice to meet you," I said.

He nodded his head and shook my hand simultaneously. Then he stood to the side so I could sit on the sofa next to Marco. "How was the ride over here?" Marco asked me immediately after he blew the cigar smoke into the air.

"It was fine."

"How is Reggie doing?"

"He's doing much better than expected," I said, trying to keep a straight face. I figured that whatever had come out of my mouth from this point had to be convincing.

"Tell me what happened?" Marco pressed the issue.

"It was simply a case of being at the wrong place at the wrong time. He was coming out of this apartment after this other guy and when a few guys from a car unloaded on the guy in front of Reggie, he messed around and got caught up in the crossfire."

"Did he have his piece on him?"

"No he didn't. Because if he did, I'm sure he would've returned fire."

"Where did he get shot?"

"He got shot once in the leg and once in the shoulder."

"So how long did they say he'll have to stay in the hospital?"

"They haven't said yet. But his wife said she'll let us know as soon as she hears something."

"Naomi, this is a serious business we are in, you agree?"

The question surprised me. I didn't know where the question came from. "Yes," I simply replied.

"Then my dear Naomi, never lie to me again," Marco said with so much confidence and surety in his voice that it brought fear to my heart.

I didn't say anything . . . primarily because I didn't know what to say.

"Naomi, I got to where I am because I keep my nose to the ground," he stated as he blew smoke again from his cigar. "Which means I know what's going on with everyone who's in my organization. I know you were robbed a few nights ago, and the guy watching your back was executed in the elevator. And before my driver picked you up, I got word that this time around Reggie was shot and is at New York Presbyterian

Hospital as we speak. I also know he was shot outside a woman's place, which means this is probably more personal than business."

Marco's dark eyes burnt through me. I knew he was allowing his words to fester inside of me. I was sure he wanted to see my reaction. Still, I kept my mouth shut. I had underestimated Marco. Something Reggie always warned me against doing. I now understood why so many people were afraid of him, and why he was in the position he was in. I had lost respect for the man because of his small ass dick. How could a man with so much money have such a little ass dick? And to think that when I used to fuck him, I acted like I loved it. Now that mistake may cost me my life. Believe me you, I was afraid but I refused to show it. My dad, Foxx told me on several occasions that my pride and my need to be in control of everything around me would get me killed. Maybe he was right after all. And tonight was probably the night I would see my fate.

"And one thing you probably don't know yet, Naomi, is two more of Reggie's locations were hit tonight while he is laid up. So now I'm wondering what is going to happen next? Is this business or personal, or a little bit of both?"

I was really fucked up right now. I didn't know if this was my last few minutes or hours to live, or what? *Why did I lie to Marco? What was going on?* It was questions I didn't have answers to. The best thing I could do was stay calm, which I was trying my best to do. But the nervousness of the unknown was kicking my ass . . . so much that I just wanted to snap my fingers and disappear.

"Don't be nervous, my little Conchita," Marco said to me. "This is a risky and deadly business we're in. And in this business people get shot. Or they'll get shot and killed. I have told Reggie this on many occasions to be straight forward no matter how crooked everyone else around him becomes because when you're dead and gone, the only thing people will remember him by is his integrity. So tell him I wish him a speedy recovery and that I will be talking to him very soon."

He took another pull on his cigar. After he blew out the smoke he immediately brought me up to speed about why I was there. I didn't have time to process one thought to the next. I had forgotten about the real man, the real Marco I first met. Evidently, he was still Marco—the man, the motherfucker who had made a serious name in this game for himself. First, he was talking shit about my dishonesty and then he flipped the fucking switch just like that to another conversation, and there was nothing I could do but listen.

"My son and I had a long talk about our operation and how we can expand it a little bit more and make a great deal of money," he continued without missing a beat. "See, Naomi, we want to bring more of our product up north since there's a market for it here. And perhaps join forces with you and your brother and take over New York City, Connecticut, New Jersey and possibly New Hampshire."

"So, how do you plan to accomplish this great feet?" I wondered aloud. I was surprised I was able to get the words out. But the curiosity of knowing what was on his mind was killing me.

"Well, I'm glad you asked," he started off and then he pulled on his cigar once more and blew out the smoke. "The fact that you work for an airline and are able to get you and your brother's product processed through Customs without it being x-rayed or inspected is magnificent. So we're proposing that if you agree to help us get Miguel's shipments through free and clear without any inspections, then we'd like to offer you five percent of the value of every delivery."

"Why don't you just pay me a set fee? Let's say, three hundred grand per load," I suggested.

He smiled and the grin developed wide over his face. He looked at his son, Miguel, who's facial expression didn't change. One minute I thought I was near death and the next I was negotiating for more cash. Foxx was right, my control issues were my biggest downfall.

"No. That's too much," Marco finally said. "We have both agreed to pay you five percent of the load's value."

"How will I know how much is being delivered?" I asked.

"You'd just have to trust what we tell you," Marco stated.

"Well, can you give me a ball park of how much would be coming though on every delivery?" I pressed the issued because I needed answers. Even though I had several TSA agents on payroll, they were sticking their necks out for me. To do what Marco and Miguel wanted to do required larger payouts. And I just couldn't go on their word that I would be told exactly how much each load would be valued at. That was a bullshit answer and Marco knew it. I wasn't as crafty as he was when it came to the drug game but I knew enough to know that he was feeding me some shit and I wasn't about to let him play me.

"Okay, listen, Marco, I'll tell you what. Let me sleep on this and get back with you in the morning. You need to realize I have TSA agents that I have to pay more money to make this work and the risk is higher. Besides, I'm tired right now. It has been a long day, and I really need to get some sleep and think about this a little more with a clearer head."

"Sure, no problem," he said as he blew smoke from his cigar again. I wanted to stuff that cigar down his fucking throat. "But while you're thinking about it, remember that this new business venture may affect the business relationship I already have with Reggie."

He winked at me and I smiled. I was tired but the wink got to me. "I will make sure I keep that in mind," I said and after that I was ready to go.

"Before you go," he stated. "Tell Damian that when a crisis like the boss getting shot happens, it's not his place to be at the hospital consoling you. He is Reggie's lieutenant-in-arms so he should be in the war zone, protecting his investments."

I was at a lost for words. I couldn't open my mouth. So I nodded my head and headed towards the front door. My mind was racing in overdrive. How dare this old motherfucker give us an ultimatum? Shit, he's basically saying that if I didn't help his son Miguel get his coke through my channels with the airline, then he was going to cut off Reggie's supply. And then to talk shit about Damian like that. That shit he was on was bogus as hell! I knew I couldn't tell him to his face what I was thinking so I thanked him for sending a driver to get me and then I told them both to have a good night.

Back at my place, I immediately got Damian on the phone. I told him everything that transpired at Marco's house and then I told him that he needed to come by my place in the morning. After he assured me he would be by to see me, we hung up.

I believe I laid in my bed for about an hour before I was able to doze off. I kept thinking about my brother. I couldn't wait until he got out of that God forsaken place and away from that dumbass wife of his. Shit, we had business to take care of. Not only did we need to find out who robbed me and killed Lucky, we also needed to find out who shot Reggie and lastly, we needed to get a handle on this shit with Marco.

I felt as if I was being backed up into a corner and I didn't like it at all. Somebody needed to do something—and do something now.

Chapter 12

Talking to the Cops

I tossed and turned all night. I didn't think I got one good wink of sleep thinking about all the shit that was going on. I looked at my alarm clock and noticed that it was a few minutes after eight, so I got up and ran two miles on my treadmill. When I was done I took a long hot shower. My mind was all over the place. I couldn't get Reggie off my mind. I needed to know how he was doing, but I dared not call his dumb ass wife. I wasn't in the mood to curse her out this morning, so I figured I'd try my chances with going back to the hospital to see him.

After I got out of the shower, I slipped on a pair of cutoff Levi denim shorts and a tight fitted t-shirt with little Ms. Hello Kitty pasted on the front of it. This was going to be a dress down day for me, so I slipped on my blue leather Gucci drivers and my blue leather Gucci bag to match. After I combed my hair back into a ponytail, I was ready to hit the street. But before I left my apartment I pulled out my Blackberry and noticed that Damian had tried to call me twice. So I dialed his number back but it kept going to voicemail, so I left him a voicemail to let him know I was on my way to the hospital to see Reggie and for him to meet me there so we could discuss a few things.

On my way to the hospital, I fumbled with how I was going to break the news to my parents that Reggie was in the hospital with a couple of gunshot wounds. My mother would probably have a nervous breakdown, but my pops would play it cool and want to know what condition he was in. But the thought of the grueling questions I would get wasn't something I was looking forward to, so I held out on the decision to call them for right now and proceeded to my destination. It was a Sunday and valet parking at the hospital wasn't available. I parked my truck back in the parking garage.

While I was getting out of my truck, my Blackberry rang. It was Damian. I pressed the send button and said, "Hello."

"I just got your voicemail about you coming up to the hospital to see Reggie," he began. "But you may want to hold out on that for a bit 'cause I just got up here a minute ago myself and when I tried to go in his room to see if he was up, I got jammed up by a couple police detectives at the door."

"What did they say?" I asked as my heart began to race.

"They asked me what my name was?"

"Did you tell 'em?"

"I had to because the other detective asked me for my ID to see if I was lying to them."

"What else did they say to you?"

"They wanted to know how I was related to Reggie. And then they asked me if I knew who shot him? But I told them I didn't know shit."

"Did you get a chance to see Reggie?"

"I saw him for a quick second."

"Was he up?"

"He was lying back, but his eyes were open."

"Did he see you?"

"Yeah, he saw me."

"Was Vanessa there?"

"I didn't see her."

"Where are you now?" I continued to question him.

"I just walked out of the hospital."

"Well, meet me on the third floor of the parking garage," I instructed him.

"Okay."

As soon as Damian reached me in the parking garage, my Blackberry rang, and it was Foxx telling me and Damian to get our asses up to Reggie's room. Before I could tell him detectives were up there, he had hung up.

I told Damian and we did as we were told.

When we reached the hallway of Reggie's room, the first person I saw was Stone standing next to the door, as if he was the bodyguard and protector of my brother. As I passed Stone, a man who has acted like my uncle since the time he and my father Foxx started hanging out back in the day, he gave me a look of disappointment. And when we entered Reggie's room, Stone stepped inside the door. I was happy to see Reggie was wide awake. Foxx was sitting in a chair next to the bed.

"How you feel," I asked my brother. He didn't immediately say anything. I felt like my world was collapsing around me. The eyes on Damian and I made me feel as if we had destroyed the world and somebody forgot to tell us.

"I shouldn't have to hear that my son was shot from Stone and anyone else," my dad spoke up. I could hear the venom in his voice. "If I expect to hear it from anyone, it should be one of you two."

Both Damian and I didn't have a comeback. I felt small and I'm sure Damian felt the same. This supposed to be a joyous occasion, but now I was sweating bullets. I felt like the damn criminal who didn't know what crime he was being convicted of.

"And your brother shouldn't have to wake up to his fucking wife complaining about him getting another woman pregnant, because his fucking sister couldn't control her fucking temper and mouth," Foxx said. Foxx rarely swore. When he did, it meant he was either very upset or disappointed, or in my case, both.

Still, I didn't say anything. What could I say? That I let a two-bit bitch get the best of me?

"Both of you, I don't need this shit," Reggie weakly stated. He raised his bed up a little. Both Damian and I were still standing at the foot of the bed. I'm sure Damian felt as I did, that we were on trial and was just finding out what the charges were.

"You," he said at me. "You should know better Naomi. You don't let anyone bait you like that, especially someone so below you like Vanessa. Come on, what in the fuck are you thinking?"

That was a question. I was now equally upset at myself because I could really see the pain Reggie was in, and I could only imagine the stress. I was really worried about his blood pressure, although the blood pressure monitor read 110 over 76. That number was 102 over 70 when we entered the room.

"And fuck Damian, two more locations were hit while your ass was here at the hospital," Reggie said in the direction of Damian.

"I ask Damian to stay with me," I immediately went to his defense.

"Naomi, just shut the fuck up for once, will you!" I was shocked. Reggie usually didn't speak this way to me. He was visibly upset. As weak as he was, his voice raised an octave.

"Damn Naomi, I spoke to Marco, and he is right, this is a fucking business, a dangerous business. If Damian is my right hand man, my lieutenant-in-arms, he does need to be out there taking care of business when I'm not around. This is serious shit we are into. It's so serious that you can be on top of the world one day, and six feet under the next."

At that point, Reggie started coughing and Foxx got up and got him some water from the water pitcher that sat on the table next to the bed. Once Reggie drank some water, he wanted to say something else, but Foxx stopped him.

"Both of you listen," Stone spoke up behind us. "Reggie needs you both. He is right about this being a dangerous business. It's a business you guys are in up to your necks. The operation has been hit three times and a fourth if you count someone taking a shot at Reggie."

Stone stopped talking and I know it was to let that point hang in the air. It was all about effect. It was then that I realized that we were in a business that we could die at a moment's notice. Hell, I should have realized that when Lucky was killed in front of me.

For a minute, I was afraid when I was with Marco and his son, and just like that, I snapped out of it when I realized Marco was going to kill me. I converted back to my old self, and that in itself was dangerous. Fuck, I had to take this seriously. After all, this was a serious business.

"Reggie will be in the hospital for a couple more days," Stone resumed speaking. "The nurse said he will be moved to the Critical Care ward tomorrow. I will be providing twenty-four hour protection for him the next couple of days. I have several cats including myself who will make sure he is not disturbed or bothered."

"What about the detectives and hospital staff?" I asked. "Wouldn't they have a problem with that?"

"No, I know people," Stone said. And that was all he had to say.

"That also includes Vanessa," Foxx stated. "I have already told her not to come to the hospital or even call. Plus, I told her that if she moves out, she better not take anything she didn't have when she first moved in."

"What about mom?" I asked.

"She knows, but she is spending time with her Aunt Trudy in Jersey City," Foxx replied. "As long as Reggie is breathing, she is happy."

I looked at Reggie and he was relaxed. His blood pressure had gone back down to a respectable 104 over 75. Inside I was elated. Reggie, Stone and Foxx had given me a lot to think about. I felt bad for Damian. He was more on the spot than me. He was the head of the business until Reggie got out of the hospital. My task was to keep my temper in check and don't let petty bitches like those bitches I work with and Vanessa get under my skin.

I was a control freak . . . and one day it might get the best of me.

Chapter 13

Dealing With Ultimatums

The tension was thick inside of Reggie's hospital room. In a way, I was still processing everything. He had four visitors in his ICU room and not one member of the hospital staff had came by to complain or run us out of there. I knew it was because of Stone. The man carried a lot of clout, but I never knew how much until now. However, the tension was getting to me. I wanted to get out of there, but I knew there were some things that needed to be discussed concerning Marco and his son Miguel, so I endured the heat.

"How long ago did you talk to Marco?" I asked Reggie.

"A few minutes before the police got here. Why?" Reggie asked in return as he repositioned his body in the bed.

"When you spoke with Marco, did he tell you about the ultimatum he gave me concerning our business venture with him?" I asked.

"Of course not. He wouldn't tell me something like that over the telephone? You know that's not how we handle our business. But we have a code setup, and he passed me the code to let me know his son Miguel would pay me a visit. Out of curiosity, what did he say?"

"He said he wanted to bring more of his supply here to the North, so Miguel can expand their operation. But they won't be able to do it unless our connections transport it through our channels."

"How much is he talking?"

"He wouldn't give me numbers. All he said was that whenever the load came through he would give me a certain percentage of the street value."

"And what percentage was that?" Reggie asked as he looked like he was grimacing in pain.

"Five percent."

"He's bullshitting you," Reggie said as a smile formed on his face. "Did you tell him we had people we had to pay to get the shit through Customs?" "Of course I did. He knows how our whole operation works. And if you want my opinion, he's not concerned about the people who make this shit happen for us. At the end of the day, all he wants is for me to call and tell him that I will make it happen for him. And if I don't, he threatens to stop your supply."

Reggie smiled again and as I looked around the room, everyone else had a smile on their face as well . . . everyone except Damian.

"What's the fucking joke because I don't get it," I spoke up and let my opinion be heard.

"He was fucking with you Naomi," Foxx stated. "He wanted to see what you were made of."

"Yeah, Marco ain't stupid, Naomi," Reggie said. "He knows how much money we have made his ass. And he knows those motherfuckers in South America can't make him the kind of money that we can. Needless to say, he needs us and we need him. But that shit he pulled with you was a test to see what you were made of, to check out your reaction."

"Why would he do some shit like that?" I asked. I was pissed off now and wanted to kick Marco's ass if that was possible.

"Because your brother is in the hospital," Stone chimed in. "And Marco needed to know that if Reggie was to die, would you be able to take over the operation. It was just a simple test to see if you had the *balls* to step up and take over."

It was something I had never thought about—Reggie dying. Even with him being shot twice, the only time I was worried was in the waiting room. But after the doctor told us he was fine and he would recover, the thought of Reggie dying left my mind. And I definitely didn't want to lose my brother, or even think about stepping up to the throne to run our operation.

"When I was at Marco's place, I was afraid he was going to kill me." It seemed as if the words had just come out on their own. I said them and it was my mouth that moved, but where the words came from, I didn't know. "He knew about you being shot and in the hospital, he knew about Lucky being killed and me being with him in the elevator, and he knew about the other two robberies that happened last night while you were here."

"Maybe Marco is behind all of this," Damian said.

Reggie looked at Damian after his statement. The room was so quiet. In fact, it was so quiet it became weird. It was apparent that everyone went into deep thought after Damian's comment.

"Both of you," Reggie said, his words directed at me and Damian. "Need to get a fucking grip. You do realize that if you weren't my sister then we would probably be planning your funeral now? You don't lie to a man like Marco . . . and both of you should know that. We're trying to get this money so we can retire. And we can't do it if everything is falling apart around us. Lying to that nigga Marco was the worst shit you could do. And Damian, you supposed to be my right hand so where in the hell are you getting shit like that from? Marco is the last motherfucker we need to be worrying about. He's a businessman. And he's only motivated when he's making dough, so why don't you get motivated and find out who is fucking with our shit! Because whoever it is, they know entirely too much and they're interrupting our flow."

"How can we be sure?" Damian asked.

"Because you, Reggie and Naomi would already be dead," Stone volunteered. "All of you started this business and you thought you could fly under the radar forever. You thought you could stay small time . . . but as soon as you started doing business with Marco the tables turned y'all are in the big leagues. The stakes are high now. And everything Reggie has done has been right. From starting up the computer store to setting up operations inside the Polo Grounds and having accounts all over the world. They were all the right moves in my eyes. *Success breeds success.* Marco would be stupid not to take advantage of a set up like that. So, no, Marco is not your problem, Damian. Your problem is someone who wants what you guys have. And the possibilities are endless. But if it was me, I would scope out the competition. And I would also look deep inside my camp. You might find out there's some unhappy cats amongst you who want to shut your operation down. And the quicker you realize who it is, the quicker you can eliminate them. Keep in mind that if they don't succeed in one way, then they could very well make that phone call to the FEDS and you don't need that."

I had a new found respect for Stone. The whole time he was talking, I kept my eyes on Foxx and Reggie. He had their undivided attention. Reggie was soaking it all in. My dad had that glow of pride in his eyes. Stone was his best friend and probably closer to Foxx than his own three brothers.

But I felt bad for Damian. In a way, he was the fall guy for all the shit happening and none of it was his fault. The shit that happened while Damian chilled with me in the waiting room while Reggie was in surgery was my fault. If there was blame for our guys getting jacked, that blame should be on me. And hell, if Damian had been there, he could have gotten shot or killed as well. In my mind, Damian didn't do shit wrong.

After Reggie gave me a few more instructions, I kissed Stone and Foxx and left the room. Damian stayed behind because Reggie wanted to speak with him. I knew Stone, Foxx and Reggie were going to chastise Damian and school him on priorities. Reggie being shot had changed the game entirely. I'm sure I wouldn't be privy to the whole new game plan. What I did know was Reggie would have a bodyguard with him at all times, including at his penthouse.

Chapter 14

Welcome to the Lion's Den

I woke up in a cold sweat. It was a nightmare, a recurring theme lately. In my bad dream, everywhere I went, I saw Lucky with his blown off face. He was stalking me, chasing me like he wanted to tell me something or worse, take me with him. Then I would have these different thoughts of Reggie being gunned down in various locations and every time he was gunned down, I was there witnessing the whole thing.

It had been two days since I had seen Reggie at the hospital. We had talked over the phone during both of those days. He assured me all was well and he asked me on several occasions, was I sure I wanted to keep doing this. Without hesitation, I told him yes.

I also let him know that I was unhappy how he, Foxx and Stone ganged up on Damian. He laughed at me and that pissed me off. But that also let me know that Reggie was getting back to being Reggie. He told me that everything was more his fault than Damian. He had gotten complacent and comfortable. He had momentarily forgotten that his head had to always be on a swivel.

And he was right. He wasn't the only one who had gotten complacent and comfortable. I think all of us had.

Today was the last day of my three days off. I wanted to do some shopping before I jumped into my housework. I was in a cleaning mood today. I wanted to do some of my domestic duties like dusting, vacuuming, sweeping, mopping, and washing clothes. The past two days when I went out, Damian had escorted me. He had come directly to my place after he left the hospital a couple of days ago and took my keys from me. It was orders from Reggie. Something told me it was probably more orders from Foxx and Stone.

I told Damian I wanted to go shopping today and he assured me he would be over early, around nine this morning.

He was a man of his word. I thought I would surprise him today. I made his favorite breakfast: steak and eggs, pancakes and toast with strawberry jam. Cooking was a forte of mine when I chose to cook. And the best thing of all was Damian loved to eat.

When I thought about that, for some crazy reason I thought about Damian eating me. One day I wanted to find out if he really did eat pussy as well as others said he did. That was crazy on my part to think of Damian that way, but hell, the man was infatuated with me, and I had grown to like him in a funny way. I knew in another life, we would probably be great together. When he knocked on the door, I made sure I had purged those thoughts from my mind. I greeted him with a kiss on the cheek. I could tell by his facial expression he was surprised. I grabbed his hand and led him to the dining room table. Then I commenced to serving him breakfast. I loved the look on his face. As he ate, I sat across from him with my ham and cheese omelet and glass of orange juice.

"Damn Naomi, this is some good ass food, girl," Damian said between bites. "I forgot you cooked like your momma." When we were growing up, Damian would come over to the house at least four days a week, and my mom was known for whipping up a pot of this or skillet of that. Both Reggie and I were miles different than our mother. But if I learned anything from moms, it was how to rule a kitchen.

Damian and I made small talk while he ate. I finished getting dress and we headed out to do some shopping. I had planned on making this a long but fulfilling day with Damian. For whatever reason, I was in a Damian mood today.

We hit all my favorite department stores in Manhattan like Barney's and Neiman Marcus and besides the occasional phone calls or texts, or Damian checking on business, I had his complete attention. While we were in Neiman Marcus he pulled out a bankroll and bought me a fifteen hundred dollar dress by Chanel. It was absolutely gorgeous. I believed I thanked him about ten times. We were friends but today I felt closer to Damian. More close to him than any man I had jumped in the sack with. I couldn't explain it. We were gelling today as if we were one—as in a couple, together.

I didn't understand it. Nor did I want to understand it. We were having a good time and I wanted to enjoy the day. This wasn't business, just two very good friends enjoying each other's company. We were *living in the moment,* and forgetting about the craziness that consumed our lives every fucking day.

Damian, Reggie and I had made some serious money in the business of selling coke, but I don't think any of us knew how much this shit would consume our lives. We lived this shit every single day of our fucking lives. So it was more than gratifying to just be enjoying the moment, the few hours we had together today. We didn't talk business. Occasionally, Damian would say something about the phone calls or texts he would receive, but I could tell he wanted so badly to just turn off his fucking phone. But he was the second in charge, and he didn't have that luxury.

After every phone call or text, he would apologize, even though I told him it was alright. I was trying to keep my mind off Damian and all of the rumors I had heard of his sexual escapades, but it was hard to do. The man really was hot too death. All the bitches in Harlem loved his black ass. He stood all of six feet tall, with a body chiseled from granite stone. The clothes he wore were always fly and accentuated his body well. He and Reggie had been inseparable since they were four years old, but I still didn't understand why he never went to college. The man graduated high school with a three point seven grade point average and had colleges falling over themselves for his service. Not only was he smart, but he was a three letter athlete, excelling in football, basketball and track. Plus, even in school, he was every young woman's dream.

While we were walking in the parking garage to get back to the car, Damian grabbed me and we ducked behind an oversized Hummer. He put his finger over his lips, meaning I needed to be quiet. I didn't have a clue what was going on. Then I heard someone say, "Where they go?"

Hearing someone ask another person about Damian and my whereabouts threw me for a loop. In my mind, I was like, what the fuck? Was someone following us? And when I looked at Damian and saw how serious his facial expression was, I damn near freaked out and I became more afraid. I wanted to open my mouth and ask him what was going on, but my mouth wouldn't move. When I realized he had a Sig Sauer in his hand, I knew the complete seriousness of this situation. It was a gold-plated Sig P226, specially made for him. I thought he was crazy when he told me he paid fifteen grand for that gun months ago.

"You two go that way, and me and Rob will go this way," I heard the leader of our followers say. Then we heard footsteps running away. I couldn't tell, but they sounded like they were only a few feet from us. Damian was in front of me as we continued to squat on the passenger side of the huge Hummer. Then we heard footsteps again but they began to walk our way.

Suddenly, and without a word to me, Damian stood up quickly and in one motion, fired off three shots. Then he grabbed me by the arm and told me to go get the car. "Hurry up and get the fuck out of here," he instructed me. I gripped my shopping bags tightly in the palm of my hands and scrambled behind one car after the next until I got to the car. It sounded like the fucking wild-wild west in the parking garage with bullets being fired back and forth and ricocheting off the walls. I didn't know which way to go but I knew I couldn't stay here, so I started up the ignition and bolted towards the exit of the parking garage like a mad woman. When Damian heard me coming, he ran out in front of the car and instead of diving through the passenger side window, he dove on top of the roof and yelled for me to keep driving. I swear, I felt like a stunt driver when I bailed out into the street. Behind us, I still heard shots being fired but I couldn't worry about that. I made sure I kept my head down and kept my feet on the accelerator and doing that I knew I had a half a chance of living.

I drove a half a block up the street and that's when Damian hopped off the hood of the car and instructed me to hurry up and pull over so he could get inside the car. After he climbed inside, he told me to be cool and don't drive like I was a fucking maniac. So once again, I did as I was told.

During the first two minutes of the drive I tried to calm myself down, but it was impossible. I had questions for Damian that I needed answered. "Who were those guys?"

"I'm not sure."

"Did you see their faces at all?"

"Yeah, I did. But I swear I've never seen them before."

"How did you know they were following us?

"I noticed them right before we went into Neiman Marcus."

"Really? Why didn't you tell me?"

"Because I knew you wouldn't have been able to handle it. You would've freaked out like you are now."

"But—" I started to say, before Damian cut me off.

"But nothing. I did what I thought was best. While you're with me, I'm gonna protect you to my last breath. You are my responsibility. So let's drop it," he replied, sounding a bit agitated. Even though I still believed I should had been forewarned about those fucking goons, I left well enough alone. Being the only woman in a male dominated drug operation, I knew my power had limits. The only power I did have was that I was in charge of my people at the airlines. But other than that, I was like third in command. I guess that's what happens when you let the men have too much fucking control.

A few minutes after Damian explained why he kept me in the dark about those goons, he pulled out his Blackberry and dialed a number. "Are you calling Reggie to tell him what happened?" I wanted to know.

"He already knew about it."

Taken aback by his reply, I looked at Damian. "When did you tell him? Where the fuck was I? I mean, damn! How come I'm the last one to know every fucking thing?" I griped.

Unfortunately, he couldn't answer my question because whomever he'd called had answered their phone. I heard their voice on the other end and quickly recognized that it was my dad, Foxx. "Tell Reggie we're okay and that we're gonna meet him at his place after I get the word that y'all have gotten there," he said and then he fell silent. I heard Foxx mumble a few words but I couldn't understand it. But then when Damian told him he'd wait for their call, I kind of figured it out. And to be sure, I put Damian's ass back on the hot seat.

"Are you going to answer my question or am I going to have to figure this shit out on my own?"

"Naomi, what do you want me to say?"

"I wanna hear the truth Damian. When did you get the chance to call and tell Reggie? And why am I always the last one to know what's going on?"

It was very obvious that Damian didn't like being questioned. He had already endured days of it from Reggie and Foxx. So to have me go in hard on him, he completely snapped. "Look, what the fuck you want me to do? Tell you a lie! Nah, I'm not that type of nigga. I'm a nigga whose suppose to protect everything and everyone around him. And remember, while you were trying on those Chanel shoes and I stepped away?"

I nodded.

"Well, that's when I called him. And from there I was given instructions to do exactly what I did. You weren't supposed to know. And if it were up to me, you wouldn't be as deep as you are in this shit now. You're a woman, Naomi. You ain't supposed to be caught up in the game like this. And if you were my wife, I would've taken you out of this shit a long time ago and put you somewhere safe so no one could ever touch you," he stated, and then he looked away from me.

Still shocked by his heartfelt openness, I honestly did not know how to react to it. This was unfamiliar territory for me. I just heard him confess his most sincere feelings for me. If we were in a less intense situation I would have laughed and dismissed his advances like all the other times when he'd confide his feelings to me. I never took him seriously. But today, something told me to stand up and take notice. I sat there with my mind going in circles as my heart sputtered, trying to discern what type of feelings I had for him.

As I tried to gather my thoughts, Damian chimed back in and said, "I haven't told Reggie this yet, but after we settle the score with the niggas who killed Lucky and finish working off this last shipment you just brought in, I'm gonna take my money and retire early."

I couldn't stay quiet any longer. My heart wouldn't let me. "What do you mean, you're retiring?" I asked.

"Naomi, I've been hustling with your brother since we were kids. Now I'm almost thirty-five, so don't you think it's time for me to retire? Settle down and start a family."

"Come on, Damian, you love the streets. So how is that going to work?" I wanted to know.

"Easy. Be my wife and I'll show you," he said.

Caught off guard once again, I was at a loss for words. I wanted to take him up on his offer but my mouth would not move. And even though I had no doubt in my mind that Damian would be the one who'd love me unconditionally and let me be me, now wasn't the time for he and I together. We had too much shit going on and too much shit to handle. So I turned my head and tried to act like he hadn't made that proposal to me. Unfortunately for me, my actions didn't work.

"Don't look away," he said as he massaged my shoulder. "You know I've wanted you for the longest.

And if you give me a chance to show you how happy I can make you, I promise you won't regret it."

"Damian, you know Reggie wouldn't approve of it."

"Who cares what he thinks? What do you want?" he pressed the issue.

"Can we talk about this some other time? My mind is going haywire right now."

"Yeah, a'ight. No problem," he replied and then he turned his attention to the people we passed by as we drove.

CHAPTER 15

Loyalty or Betrayal

After five minutes of deafening silence, my Blackberry rang. It was Reggie again, but this time he called my phone. I answered on the second ring and he told me to put it on speaker.

"You a'ight?" Reggie asked.

"I've been better, but I'm good," Damian responded.

"Well, I called to let y'all know that there's been a change of plans. Marco is sending Miguel by the house in the next hour, so instead of meeting me at our spot, meet me at the house," Reggie instructed us, so I made a left at the next traffic light so I could switch up the route.

"Have you left the hospital yet?" I asked.

"Yeah, I'm in the car with Foxx and Stone now. I'm gonna send Vanessa out to fill my prescriptions before Miguel gets there."

"Okay, well we're on our way there now."

"A'ight. Cool. But first, I'm gonna need y'all to make a quick stop to this spot in Harlem," he said.

"Sure, where?"

Reggie laid out everything concerning this endeavor. Damian and I had to check on these cats and it was very imperative that it got done today. "We're on it. So answer your phone, because as soon as we get out there, be on alert 'cause we're gonna call you right back."

"I'll be waiting," he stated.

After I stuck my phone back into my handbag, we changed our direction and headed to Harlem like Reggie had instructed us to do. We rode in complete silence, even though my heart wanted to let down my guard and give in to Damian. I knew I was being a fool. But I wasn't the first and nor would I be the last who failed to jump on true love when it was presented to me—in the right package with the right man. But like all fools, I hope I wouldn't regret my decision one day.

Ben and Dre lived together in the Polo Grounds. I picked up my speed but made it a point not to go more than eight or nine miles pass the speed limit. Besides the phone call, the SUV had been quiet. I couldn't tell you why we weren't talking, but Damian's mind was elsewhere. I could only assume it was on the punk ass niggas who tried to kill us earlier. That's what I told myself. But I knew he was probably thinking about me—about us. I hope he wasn't thinking about the future—without the streets, *without me.*

"Thanks for saving my ass in the parking garage, Damian," I said to break the silence. I was appreciative and thankful for Damian being there. "Were they out to kill or kidnap me?"

"That was a hit, baby girl," Damian said in a low voice. "And I'm wondering who in the fuck was bold enough to run up on me like I didn't matter," he continued. "This wasn't just about you, it was about us.

They wanted me gone just as bad as they wanted you gone."

I was driving and I looked over at Damian, and he returned the look. This wasn't just about me, or Damian. This was about hurting Reggie.

Silence once again captured my truck. And of all the thoughts that came to mind, I thought about Damian and the fact that he called me—*baby girl.* I absolutely loved when Damian called me *baby girl.* It always sounded affectionate and warm when he called me that. It was evident that he loved me and my heart knew that I would take him up on his proposal just as soon as this whole ordeal was over. I mean, who knows, I may even retire myself. I'd love to go away with Damian and start a family.

We were two minutes from the Polo Grounds when I surprised Damian with a question. "Do you think you killed any of those guys you shot back there inside of the parking garage?"

He looked at me with a bit of shock on his face. Just by the gleam in his eyes, I knew he didn't want to talk about this. "Naomi, that's not an appropriate question to ask a man, and that's the perfect way to become a witness to a crime. And you wouldn't be ready for that."

"Yeah, a'ight," I said and then I left the subject alone. And the rest of the drive was done in complete silence.

The great thing about the spot where Ben and Dre lived was that you could get lost inside one of the towers. Although the Polo Grounds wasn't as big as all the other projects in the city, its size still created its own massive maze. When I pulled up to the first tower I noticed cop cars as well as news station vans occupying the parking lot. As with anything else that happened in the hood, the hood chicks were all over the place as well. It was obvious that whatever happened, occurred in tower one. The same tower I was held up in. The same tower Lucky was killed in.

When we arrived, Ben and Walt met us in the door and another one of Reggie's guys I barely knew held the elevator door for us. Walt didn't make eye contact with me. I didn't know if he felt ashamed for the shit that happened to me, or was just afraid to say anything to me because of the shit that went down. He looked haggard, run down. Something told me this wasn't the gig for him.

When we reached the tenth floor, the elevator stopped and we all got off. Ben told Walt to man the elevator, and we proceeded to Ben and Dre's place. Ben knocked on the door two times, hesitated several seconds, and then rapped the door three more times. At that point, Dre opened the door and we all walked inside.

I couldn't believe my fucking eyes when I walked deep inside the apartment. In the kitchen was a young brother, maybe in his late teens or early twenties, tightly tied to a kitchen chair with duct tape. He also had duct tape over his mouth. His face was puffy and bloody from the beating he had endured from probably both Ben and Dre. To make matters worse, there was plastic underneath the chair and spread out over the floor. All of that signified one thing—his death was numbered in minutes, not days, or hours.

"I'll be damn, say it isn't so," Damian stated.

"What?" I said out of curiosity.

"You don't recognize the kid?" Damian asked.

I looked at the young blood again and couldn't make out the face. His face was too fucked up for me to make a proper identification.

"It's Lil Man," Damian volunteered. "We've known this nigga since he was about thirteen. We took his ass underneath our wing and taught him how to fight and take care of himself."

I did remember the kid Damian was talking about. I was surprised at how he had grown. He was still short, maybe standing about five six, but his body had filled out.

Dre took the stage and told us what had happened. In three minutes or less, he had told us that Candie had missed one of her check in times, which was something Reggie had required everyone to do after what had happened with Lucky and I. Candie had no problems with the new rule. In fact, we never had a problem with her sticking to the rules. She was supposed to check in every hour on the hour. Up until now she had done just that, so everyone who held down this particular tower became suspicious. Ben and Dre immediately went to her place and saw the door kicked in. And that's when the shooting began. Come to find out, Lil Man's accomplice almost escaped but he had been shot at least six times. He ran down the staircase and died in front of the tower. Lil Man wasn't shot, but when he ran out of bullets, Ben and Dre beat the shit out of him, and brought him to their apartment. If anyone saw them dragging him from one building to the next, they knew not to say anything. That was the power of being in power.

Unfortunately, Lil Man and his accomplice had beat Candie half too death. I had mad respect for the woman because she refused to give them motherfuckers the money she had made.

Damian had me dial Reggie's number and Reggie told us he would call us right back on my phone. His theory was if the cops were bugging anyone's phone, they wouldn't bug my phone. I was an innocent . . . or so they thought. When the phone rang right back, I didn't know the number but I answered anyway. It was Reggie using one of the nurse's phones. Why wasn't I surprised?

My phone was on speaker. Damian explained quickly what was going down and it didn't take Reggie any time getting in the mix. "Damn, Lil Man, we treated your ass righteous. Made sure no one fucked with you, and even gave you money to help out your family. We made sure your ass stayed out of trouble and this is how you pay us back."

I could actually hear the disappointment in Reggie's voice. I didn't have a good feeling about this. We had passed crazy as hell a long time ago. This was some surreal shit and I couldn't believe I was here in the middle of it. Usually, I just heard about all of the real crazy shit that happened in our business. Now I was a witness.

"So tell me, Lil Man, who are you working for?" Reggie asked.

Dre pulled the duct tape from Lil Man's mouth. He let out a yelp and it took him several seconds to get himself together. Then he surprised the shit out of us when he said, "Com' on, Reg, you know who put me up to this. Who else do you think I would do some crazy shit like this for? It was your homeboy, Damian! That's who!"

I damned near jumped out of my skin when Lil Man made that announcement. That was the last thing I expected him to say. Damian was shocked by his answer to. He acted like he was two seconds from whipping his ass like Ben and Dre had just done. But I was glad Reggie didn't buy what he was selling.

"Help me out, Lil Man . . . what am I gonna do with you?" Reggie said jokingly. I noticed I was the only one shocked or took what Lil Man said seriously. "This is what we are gonna do. Dre, get the kit out." Dre went into the bathroom, while Reggie kept talking. "Last time, Lil Man. You know I don't like asking the same question twice, but since we have history, I will be nice and nicely ask you again, who are you working for?"

I noticed the sweat that had formed on Lil Man's face. I saw a slight glimmer of confidence in his eyes. He actually thought he was onto something.

"I told you, Reg, and I wouldn't lie to you, you know that man. It was your fucking homeboy who is trying to play it cool right now. Your right hand man, Damian."

I noticed Damian didn't open his mouth. But he looked like he wanted to hurt Lil Man really bad. If it was me and I was innocent, I would be screaming at the top of my lungs that this motherfucker was lying. But Damian just stood there and looked at Lil Man.

They were having an old-fashioned stare down, and I wondered who would blink first.

When Dre came back, Reggie said, "Damian, you know what to do. It's your show, my brotha."

"I got it, Reggie," Damian said without hesitation. He was calm, cool and collected. With each minute that passed, my respect and admiration grew for Damian. And I still didn't know what that was about.

"Last chance, dumbass, who paid you?" Damian asked.

Lil Man smiled and told Damian to go fuck himself.

"Say no more nigga!" he replied sarcastically and then he turned his attention to Dre and instructed him to pull out the hedge clippers and cut off the trigger finger on both hands.

Lil Man's eyes got big and he was about to scream, but Ben beat him to it. Ben hit him hard across his lip, possibly hitting his teeth because his gums started bleeding and then re-taped his mouth. Then I stood there and watched as Ben held his hands still, while Dre cut off Lil Man's fingers. First, the right hand, then the left. Then Dre pulled out salt from the makeshift first aid kit that they aptly named the kit. This was so far from a first aid kit. After pouring the salt on his wounds, Damian then pulled out the rubbing alcohol and poured half the bottle over the two cut fingers.

If Lil Man hadn't almost killed Candie, then maybe I would have had some sympathy for him. But I didn't. For all I knew, he was probably the one who had shot Reggie. That thought alone made me want to pick up something and fuck him up.

I noticed the tears running wild down Lil Man's face. I could only imagine the pain he was feeling. And they were just getting started.

"Pull the tape from his mouth," I said to no one in particular.

Damian looked at me but he didn't say anything. He did what I said.

"Lil Man, I do remember you. You were a nice young man. I remember you eating over our house and running errands for my dad. Whoever is behind all this, are they really worth you dying? Hell, what you gonna do now. You have no trigger fingers and you know these motherfuckers out here will try to make an example out of you."

"It . . . it . . . it was Wa . . . Walt."

Immediately, Ben and Dre ran out the door to get Walt, but they returned within a couple of minutes. Walt was nowhere to be found. They called his number and it went straight to voicemail. They called and talked to the guys downstairs and everyone else in the four towers, and no one had seen the motherfucker.

Reggie told Damian to do what was necessary. It was then I noticed everyone had latex gloves on except me. I didn't know if Lil Man could hear the clock of death ticking loudly in his head, but I sure could.

Damian asked him a couple more questions and I believed Lil Man told the truth. Walt was the front man, not the HNIC. Someone else was calling the shots. Plus, he swore that he wasn't involved in Reggie's shooting.

When Ben was about to put the tape back over Lil Man's mouth, he said, "Damian, this ain't right, man. You don't know what you are doing."

"How so?" Damian asked.

"I'm a member of AFH and they won't let me die in vain."

"So, that's the reason no one has heard from you in a while," Damian stated. "So you are one of them motherfuckers, huh? Well, I guess all of fucking Harlem is at war . . . and guess what, round one goes to us."

With that, Ben put the tape over Lil Man's mouth, then Damian, Ben and Dre huddled up around each other. I heard Damian talking but I couldn't make out what he said.

When we left, Lil Man's eyes were filled with tears and I understood his fear. I asked Damian who and what was AFH?

"AFH is short for Assassins For Hire," he replied. "They are a gang of about fifteen young cats who kill for money, usually in Harlem only. But maybe they are branching out. I think I shot a couple of them niggas in the parking garage."

Inside the elevator, I couldn't help but draw near him, so I walked over to him and laid my head on his chest and he hugged me. I knew now that he was my security blanket. I had objected when Reggie first told me that Damian would be by my side from here on out because of the shit that happened. Now I wanted him to never leave my side. I felt safe with him around.

CHAPTER 16

Back at Headquarters

Once again, we were back on the road, but this time we were en route to Reggie's place. I asked Damian what would happen to Lil Man. I don't know why I asked. I knew whatever they had planned would end with one result—Lil Man's death. When Damian told me they would wait until later, then take Lil Man to the roof of their tower and let him sail downward while still tied up to the chair, made me realize I really was in deep.

I didn't know how to feel. I was numb. My own brother, Reggie, was the kingpin of this operation—and I was his partner, along with our best friend, Damian. Now we were being hunted, and worse, we were killing folks as well. *Whatever happened to this being a simple operation? What happened to just a little supply and demand?* That's how Reggie sold me on this crazy ass shit, *a little supply and demand.*

Trying to take in the shit that happened to Lil Man and then heading over to Reggie's apartment to have the meeting with Miguel had begun to take a toll on me. Luckily, I had taken time off at work. I knew if I hadn't, then I'd be a nervous wreck trying to service our airline's passengers and deal with the other bitches I worked alongside with. On many levels I took my job seriously, so I was very fortunate to be able to take a leave of absence for a few days to handle my affairs at home.

When we arrived at Reggie's building, we had valet park my SUV. Then we headed up to the penthouse floor. To my surprise, Vanessa was very pleasant with Damian and me when she answered the door.

"Hola, Mommie!" she greeted me. "And how are you Damian?" she continued, as she let us inside the luxury apartment.

I swear I didn't know how to take her happy-go-lucky routine. In actuality, Vanessa was a mean bitch eighty-five percent of the time, so for her to act like she was excited to see us was weird. In fact, I knew she was being phony, but I went along and played her game with her. I even went as far as hugging her and giving her a kiss on her cheek. Damian looked at me like I was crazy.

"Where's the man of the house?" I asked.

"He and Foxx are in the bedroom, but they'll be out in a minute. Go to the den area and wait for them."

"A'ight. Thanks," Damian replied and then he followed me towards that area of the penthouse, while I followed behind Vanessa.

I looked back at Damian and gave him a funny expression while Vanessa wasn't looking. He smiled back at me and shook his head like he knew what time it was. "Y'all want something to drink?" she asked after we entered into the den area.

"Nah, I'm straight," Damian spoke up first.

"Yes, I'm fine too. I just had a sixteen ounce bottle of water on my way here," I lied and then I took a seat on my brother's white leather sofa. Damian sat next to me.

"Well, just let me know if y'all change your minds," she replied as she stood in the middle of the floor showing off her Python print sling back Christian Louboutin heels. Even though I couldn't stand the sight of this snake ass bitch, she wore the hell out of those shoes. And to sport the Python print satin blouse and a belt to accessorize with the tan linen shorts she had on was really hot! One thing I could say about the slut was that she was a miserable ass- hole, but she knew how to spend my brother's money. She took advantage of Reggie's cheating by going on serious shopping sprees to make herself feel better. She even took money from his emergency stash a few times after she learned or suspected him of cheating. That was why Reggie got the other spot, to keep her slimy paws off his loot. He kept his money there. And Damian and I were the only ones who knew about it.

While Ms. Gold-digger stood front and center so Damian and I could look her over, Foxx finally escorted Reggie into the room. It was then that it hit me that when our mom or dad was around, then Vanessa would go into that nice daughter-in-law routine. I laughed inside because both my mom and dad knew she was a money grubbing bitch, who didn't know the meaning of the word love.

Reggie's shoulder and left leg were bandaged. He was moving around gingerly. While Foxx was getting him situated on the love seat across from us, Vanessa walked over to them and acted like she was concerned for his well well-being. "Baby, think you're gonna need a pillow for your back?" she asked.

Reggie knew she was putting on an act in front of everyone, especially for Foxx, so he played along with her. I'm sure he figured if he went along with her game, then he'd be able to have a little more peace than normal. "Yeah, but get me that small black pillow on our bed. That one would probably work better than all the other pillows we've got," he told her.

"Okay," she said and then she left the room.

Damian and I looked at each other again right after she left the room. "She's so fucking fake! It's ridiculous," I mumbled loud enough for only Damian to hear me.

While Vanessa was in the bedroom, Reggie started in on a conversation. "I'm glad y'all made it here in one peace."

"Me too," I chimed in.

"Yeah, it was rough at first, but we came out of it," Damian added.

"You don't think no one followed y'all back here, do you?" Foxx wanted to know. I loved my dad but he was nothing like his best friend, Stone. Stone was a very adequate name for Uncle Stone. Nothing fazed that damn man. But Foxx was overcautious and always on alert. I couldn't complain though. He had only spent one stint in prison for three years and that was saying something for a man who had been running the streets for over fifty-five years.

"Nah, because after we got away from that run in, we made a detour and went straight out to the Polo Grounds."

"So, you don't think no one followed you after you left the Polo Grounds to come here?" Reggie wanted to know.

"Nah, nobody followed us," Damian said adamantly.

"What about Ben and Dre? They handled their business tonight?" Reggie continued.

"Yeah, they put in the required work. It just messed me up to see that Lil Man was down with that shit that went down," Damian said.

I sat there and remained quiet. I had no knowledge of the relationship Reggie and Damian had with Lil Man. Nor did I want to know, especially after what I witnessed tonight. While they discussed bits and pieces of what transpired tonight, Vanessa walked her grimy ass back in the room and placed the black pillow Reggie had requested behind his back. Two seconds later, their door bell rung. Everyone in the room knew it had to be Miguel, but no one opened their mouth to actually say it. Reggie instructed Vanessa to answer the door.

After she went to let Miguel in, I got up from my chair, told them to excuse me and then I went to the bathroom located in the nearby hallway. I had to get away for a moment so I could clear my mind and douse my face with some cold water before I came face-to-face with Miguel again. He wasn't like his father Marco, but I could tell that he was a piece of work. And if he was anything like his father, I knew when he stepped into that back room with us, then he would mean business.

By the time I got out of the bathroom he had already entered the room and greeted everyone, including Foxx. I heard all of their voices loud and clear. I started to exit the bathroom so I could enter back into the den and make Miguel aware of my presence, but I decided that I'd wait just a few more minutes. I wanted to hear how Reggie would handle Miguel's shipment situation without my involvement. After I sat down on the side of the toilet stool, I heard an earful. Miguel's English was much better than his father's, so it wasn't hard to follow their conversation at all.

"Naomi is taking care of business in another room but she'll be out in a moment," Reggie said.

"What you and I need to discuss doesn't require her presence," Miguel stated.

"Well, let's begin then," I heard Reggie say. Then I heard Miguel start up by saying that he and his father had a lot of new territory that needed to be supplied and in order to do that they needed me to make a way for his shipments to come through my channels at least twice a month.

"That part I'm already aware of Miguel. What I need to know now is how much is coming through? Remember, the amount of product you're requiring to come through Naomi's channels will determine how much manpower we'll need. We can't have a half of ton of product coming through and we have only three men working the site. With a load like that we'll need at least two or three extra men. And with more manpower comes more payout."

"If the products are packaged inconspicuously then we wouldn't need all of that manpower," Miguel suggested.

In my mind, it was obvious that Miguel was trying to find a way to get out of telling Reggie how much was coming in, so he wouldn't have to pay us more to make sure it got through our channels without any interruptions. Little did he know, Reggie wasn't going for that bullshit he was throwing our way. Reggie was more of a businessman than he'd ever be, so he'd better step up to the plate and come correct.

"The way our operation works, it really doesn't matter how the load is packaged up," Damian chimed in. "We, and the folks in our employ, take the risk. We ensure they get paid and they ensure we get our product. If not, they could possibly have thoughts about getting the shipment intercepted so they could keep it for themselves. Then what do we do? Kill them . . . and hope we can find other employees who are as cool as they were? That's why it's important for you to have extra manpower in the loop. That way the men who are put in charge to make sure the loads get through can and will be watched by the extra men we have lurking behind the scenes and undetected."

I had to admit that Damian impressed me the way he stepped in and had Reggie's back. I'm sure Reggie appreciated it as well. I had to remember they had been friends for thirty damn years and probably knew how each other thought. I waited for Miguel come to back at them with more of his slick as talk but he remained quiet. I figured he was trying to figure out how to negotiate with Reggie and Damian without giving them too much power. I sat back in the bathroom and laughed my butt off because I knew that he felt somewhat powerless in this group of three men. I guessed now he knew how I felt when he and Marco had my ass backed up against the wall while I was on their territory.

"Listen, Miguel, I'm a businessman, so I don't mind doing this new venture. But you and Marco gotta' cut us some slack," I heard Reggie say. "When we take on a job we don't do it half ass! We stand behind everything we do. That's why it's important for us to know the exact weight of the load, so we can get the right people in place. Plus, we need the necessary capital to pay them . . . because at the end of the day, we're paying them to protect a much larger investment."

"How much do you want?" Miguel asked.

"See, you're missing the point," Reggie replied quickly. "I can't tell you how much money it'll take to get your product through until you tell us how much weight you're getting shipped."

"Well, I'ma tell you right now that that's not going to happen. When we used to use cargo ship containers to get out product out of South America, or use mules to transport it from one state to the next, we never told them how much they were carrying. It was none of their business. The only thing they needed to worry about was getting it to its destination safely. That's it. So, the same rules apply here."

"Okay, listen, I'll tell you what, Miguel," Reggie retorted, "if you and Marco agree to pay us $300,000 per shipment, which I think is more than fair considering you could maximize each load by shipping anywhere between one hundred and fifty to two hundred kilos at a time and come off lovely. Because if you look at it from a profit standpoint, you can sell each kilo for twenty-eight to thirty grand wholesale and end up with over five and a half million easy. So three hundred grand is a drop in the bucket when you look at all the money you stand to make."

I waited for Miguel to speak. But for the first thirty seconds he didn't say anything. I figured he was doing the math in his own head and wanted to be sure about the figures Reggie was throwing at him. At this point in the conversation, I wished I was there so I could see the look on his face.

"If I agree to pay you three hundred thousand dollars, I can ship as much product as I want?" Miguel finally spoke up.

Reggie started laughing. Apparently he thought Miguel was either being humorous or he was trying to insult him. I couldn't stand being in the bathroom anymore. I felt like I had to get in on the conversation with Miguel and Reggie, so I got up from the toilet and opened the bathroom door. It startled me to see Vanessa standing next to the door. She literally scared the shit out of me, which of course made me jump back. "You scared me too death!" I said.

Being that she wasn't expecting to see me coming out of the bathroom only to catch her eavesdropping on my brother's business deal, she didn't know how to carry herself. Her body language was totally off. "I'm sorry. I didn't know you were in there," she said quietly. It was evident that she didn't want Reggie to hear our conversation.

"I was trying to use the bathroom but I couldn't," I told her.

"I'm glad you came out first, because I was getting ready to come in there myself," she continued saying, trying to convince me that she was only there for a couple of seconds. But she knew I knew what time it was with her. So I did the noble thing and tried my best to make her feel less awkward.

While Vanessa tried to paint the picture that she was so glad that she hesitated before she walked into the bathroom so I wouldn't go back and tell Reggie the real deal, I heard Reggie reiterate to Miguel that he could send as much coke in at a time, but it couldn't weigh over one ton, especially at the price he was paying us. And once Miguel understood Reggie's terms, he finally agreed to them.

Before I could get back into the room, Miguel told Reggie that he wanted us to make the proper arrangements. He wanted his first shipment to come in one week from today. Reggie knew he couldn't make that judgment call, because that was my area of expertise. He knew I only scheduled shipment deliveries on the days I worked. When he yelled my name and told me to come back to the den, I knew he needed me to give Miguel the green light.

I patted Vanessa on the back and told her to stop explaining and that I was fine and then I walked off. When I entered back into the den, all eyes were on me. Reggie quickly brought me to speed about how he and Miguel came to an agreement about the figures, so the deal had been made. Now he needed me to shed light on whether or not Miguel would be able to get his first shipment in one week from today? Since I had already heard the question from the hallway, I had time to think if I worked next Tuesday. I looked at Reggie and Miguel both and told them what they wanted to hear.

"Yes, I work next Tuesday, so that would be fine. All I need to know is whether or not you'd rather ship your load in the morning or at night?"

"The earlier, the better," Miguel said.

"Okay. I'm on it," I assured him.

Since he was already standing up when I entered the room, he walked over to me and kissed me on both cheeks. "I look forward to doing business with you," he said.

"Likewise," I replied.

After he wished Reggie a speedy recovery, Damian escorted him out of the apartment and downstairs to the car that was waiting for him.

Chapter 17

Got More $ Than I Can Count

While Damian was downstairs with Miguel, I took this opportunity to talk to Reggie about this new venture. I took a seat on the sofa across from Reggie and Foxx and started off by letting them know that I heard their entire conversation and how impressed I was when Damian stepped in to help sway the negotiations. The only question I had for him was did he think three hundred grand was enough money for all the risk we had to take?

"Put it like this, a nigga could never pay us enough money to do what we do. But in this situation, I believe that we can make it work," Reggie replied.

"You know we're cutting it close by allowing him to get his shipment in one week from today. Normally, I would need at least ten days to get the proper paperwork put in the system, get the shipping labels and make sure that my men are on the schedule for that day."

"Why didn't you tell us that when we asked you?" Reggie asked.

"Because when I entered into the room I felt the pressure for me to say yes."

"Come on now, Naomi, that's not how we handle business."

"I know this. But can you take some of the blame for putting me on the spot?"

"Nah, I'm not gonna do that. You're a business-woman. It's your job to run the shipping and handling part of our operation. So when someone ask you if they can have their product delivered one week from today, when you know that it takes at least a week and a half to orchestrate a proper delivery, then you need to speak up and let them know. Otherwise, you're gonna be 'round here running around with your head in too many places and you're bound to drop the ball. And in this business, we can't afford for you to do that. There are too many people's lives at stake. Not only that, it's hard to buy freedom, so please keep that in mind."

I shook my head and let out a long sigh. I couldn't take it when Reggie put me on the hot seat and scolded me like I was his fucking child. Shit, was it wrong that I only said yes to please Miguel? I mean, I was just at a meeting with him and Marco a couple days ago when they first gave me the ultimatum, have his product delivered at a set fee or else. So Reggie needed to get off my back and cut me some slack.

Instead of going back and forth with Reggie about how I should have handled the situation with Miguel, I sat there quietly and tried to figure out who I needed to get on the phone first, so I could make this first delivery run smoothly.

While I was in deep thought, Foxx said a few words to me. "Listen, baby girl, I know you think your brother is coming down hard on you, but you gotta remember that he's only pointing these things out to you because he doesn't want you to fail. Y'all got a lot of shit at stake. So you can't afford to mess up at this point in the game. One small fuck up could cause you to lose everything you've worked so hard to get. And I'm sure you don't want that."

I didn't know if it was a question or a statement, I answered anyway, "Of course I don't."

"Well, get yourself together and stop sitting there like the whole world is on your shoulders," Foxx continued.

"I'm good," I assured them both and then I pulled my Blackberry out and dialed my point of contact, which happened to be one of the TSA agents I had on my payroll. I didn't have any intentions to talk about Miguel's shipment; I just wanted to let him know that we needed to have a sit down before nightfall. When I finally got him on the phone and he confirmed that he'd be able to meet up with me when his shift was over at ten tonight, I gave him the exact time and location where to meet me. Immediately after I ended our call, I assured Foxx and Reggie that I was going to meet up with one of my guys to get the ball rolling and that everything would be okay. Once I made them understand that I intended to make up for that bad judgment call I made earlier.

"One more thing," I said. "Damian didn't get a chance to tell you, but Lil Man said he worked for a gang called AFH."

Reggie and Foxx looked at each other with stunned looks on their faces. I didn't know what to make of it, but I didn't have long to wait to find out.

"Shit, someone really wants you dead, son," Foxx said matter-of-factly. But I could see the concern on his face. "No one knows who these kids are, but they supposed to be some crazy, whacked out ass kids. Word is they burned and shot two crackheads who raped a middle school girl in Harlem. Supposedly the family only gave them five grand to whack both of them."

I looked at Reggie and I could tell he was intently listening to Foxx. Regardless of how overly cautious Foxx could be, Reggie knew when he needed to pay attention to the old man.

"Good possibility they were the ones who tried to kill y'all at the mall," Reggie said. "I think we need to increase security for everyone." Reggie stopped and looked at Foxx. I already knew what he was about to say and I know it was going to hurt him to say the words. "Foxx, you and Mom need to go to Philly and spend some time with Uncle Jimmie until this shit is dead."

I saw the intensity on both of their faces. Foxx didn't want to go. But he knew it wasn't about him, it was about his wife, our mother.

"I'ma do that," Foxx replied. "I will get Stone to follow us, then give him the keys to the house. Plus, I'ma have Stone run down who these kids are."

"Then what?" I interrupted.

"What you mean?" Foxx asked in return.

"What will Stone do after he finds out who they are?" I asked stupidly.

Foxx smiled and a smirk came across the face of Reggie. "Baby, I don't ask Stone what he does. I tell him the problem and he makes the problem go away. Sometimes the problem is never seen again. Other times, if I do see the problem again, it's months or years later. But guess what . . . the problem is solved."

It didn't take much to realize the *problems* my dad was referring to were people. Stone always had my dad's back. It was a matter of Foxx opening his mouth and asking Stone to resolve the problem. I was wishing Reggie had that clout with Stone. But something told me, Damian was Reggie's version of Stone.

"Tell Damian that I don't want him to leave your side," Reggie spoke up. "Hell, it would be better if you guys went to a hotel and got a suite, but if you decide to stay in your place, make sure he sleeps in the living room where he can hear everything."

I nodded in the affirmative; then I kissed them both and excused myself. While I was making my way to the front door, Vanessa met me in the foyer.

"Leaving so soon?" she asked.

"Yeah, I've got a few errands to run before I head home."

"Can't you stay just a little longer? I just started a pot of my spicy red chicken with my famous chili sauce and I would love for you to take some of it home with you."

"Why don't you save some of it in a bowl for me and I will stop by and pick it up tomorrow," I lied. Truth is, I could care less about eating anything she cooked. For all I knew, she could have been trying to poison my ass. Especially since I rained on her parade at the hospital when I told her about the baby Reggie was supposed to have on the way. She couldn't fool me. I saw right through her sneaky ass. Better luck next time bitch.

By the time I got downstairs, Damian was just leaving the valet area. I walked up to him after he reentered the building.

"What the hell you been doing all this time?" I didn't hesitate to ask.

"I was talking to Miguel."

"About what?" I pressed the issue.

"Can you believe he offered me a job to come work for him?"

I took a step back to take in what Damian had just dropped on me. "How did he offer you a job? What did he say?" I asked.

"He mentioned that he liked how I laid out all the cards on the table for him. He said that I gave him better insight on how our operation ran. And because of it, he felt like I could be trusted."

"So you're telling me that he asked you to jump ship and get down with his organization because you seem like you can be trusted? Come on now, you gotta' be leaving something out of this conversation. Miguel and Marco are some hard-nose ass characters and they don't just let anyone in their circle. So come clean."

Damian grabbed me by my arm and pulled me into an isolated corner of the building's lobby area. "I can't for sure, but after having that talk with Miguel, I believe that the only reason he offered me a job to be his right hand man is so that I can help him expand his operation. In his mind, he wants to be the primary supplier in these northern states. So you know what that mean?"

"Yeah, it means that if we help him bring his product here, then it's just a matter of time before he takes over and runs Reggie out of business."

"Exactly."

"So what did you tell him?"

"What do you think I told him?" he responded sarcastically. "I told him I appreciated the offer but my loyalty was with Reggie."

"And what did he say?"

"He gave me a card with his number on it and told me to use it if I ever changed my mind."

I shook my head with disgust. "That grimy motherfucker is unbelievable. They take us through all that bullshit and lowball us with their measly ass three hundred grand so we can bust our asses to get their shit here and for what? So they can end up beating our prices and eventually take over? That's bogus if you ask me."

"Yeah, it is. But that shit he's trying to do goes with the territory Naomi. So, don't get all bent out of shape about it. Remember, we got enough money to retire now. So if push comes to shove, that's what we'll do."

"What about Reggie? Don't you think we should tell him?"

"Don't worry. I will. But before we do that, let's make sure those are Miguel's intentions."

"Alright."

Chapter 18

Roll Call

My head TSA agent name was Evan. He met up with me and Damian last night as planned and he assured us he wouldn't have a problem processing the paperwork on short notice. He was convinced he could get the proper shipping labels and his guys ready in time for Miguel's shipment. I was very pleased to hear that. Money was a helluva motivator for him.

The only other loose end I needed to tie up was to get my other men in place, so they could keep a watchful eye out on Evan and his boys. I've learned that you could never have too many niggas watching other niggas, just to make sure they're doing their job.

So Damian and I headed to the airport. I had to work a late flight with Sabrina and two other flight attendants for a one o'clock flight to DC. It was only a few minutes after nine and since I had a couple of hours to play around with, I headed over to the TSA Administration Office, where I needed to speak with my law enforcement connection. I told Damian that I was safe now. I was in my territory and with airport security the way it is now since 9/11 years ago, someone had to be beyond stupid to bring weapons to the airport with all of the law enforcement at New York's airports. Young or not, I didn't think even those young ass street niggas were that stupid.

Damian kissed me on the cheek as he gave me my house and car keys. He jumped in a taxi and I couldn't take my eyes off the taxi as it drove off. I really didn't know what was going on with me and Damian, but that motherfucker was under my skin and for whatever reason, I was still having reservations about that. I didn't know if it was because of Reggie or was I the problem.

I slept in a spare bedroom in case those young ass gang members came looking for me and somehow managed to scale the wall like fucking Spiderman and climbed through my window. If they were that ambitious, I didn't want to be in the obvious place. Amazingly, Damian didn't sleep on the sofa in the living room. He made a makeshift bed on the floor in the hallway outside my spare bedroom. I think that act of chivalry was what kept my pussy moist the whole fucking night.

He was awake when I fell off to sleep . . . and awake when I woke up this morning. I really don't think he slept at all last night. I was so fucking tired from motherfuckers shooting at us to dealing with Lil Man's ordeal at the Polo Grounds, then dealing with Miguel and that trifling bitch, Vanessa. On top of all that, my parents were now in Philly until all of this shit blew over. But instead of being worried the whole night, I slept like a fucking log. How crazy was that?

Instead of going through the front entrance of the TSA Administration Office, I walked outside on the tarmac and went in through the back. For our particular airline, the federal government hired over one hundred federal marshals and law enforcement officers to work undercover to prevent future terrorist attacks on our homeland. It was a shame I had access to four of those law enforcement officers when I needed a job done. I wondered what the federal government would say about that shit. Under my breath, I thanked the fucked up economy and recession for making even the unimpeachable vulnerable for more money.

"Well, good morning, Mr. Wright," I said the moment I walked in the back office. Mr. Wright was the head LEO for the airport. He was my go-to-man because he had been working for this division since they implemented it back when George Bush was President. Mr. Wright had to be in his late forties. I liked the way he handled business. Although he was a black man with over one hundred law enforcement officers under his command, he didn't let the power go to his head. The man knew his shit and no one fucked with him. But like any average motherfucker today, he needed extra money for his family and bill collectors.

"I'm just great. What about you?" he smiled. His teeth were pearly white and his mustache had a nice mix of salt and pepper hair added to his distinction. With a million dollar smile, he sort of reminded me of the late Gerald Levert, but with a little more height.

I walked around his desk and extended a hug to him. "I'm good," I smiled back. "Are you working alone today?" I continued to question him as I checked out the surveillance cameras he was monitoring.

"For right now I am. John went to get him a breakfast sandwich and a cup of coffee. He'll be back in a few minutes. Why? Do you need to talk to me?"

"Why of course I do."

"Have a seat," he insisted. I took a seat in the chair behind the other desk that was only a few feet away from him.

After I sat down, I immediately went into why I was there to see him. "I've got another shipment coming through next Tuesday and I'm gonna need you and John or maybe Rick to come on board."

"What time is it scheduled to come in?"

"In the morning."

"Who you got working the floors and bringing it through?"

"Evan and his crew."

Mr. Wright thought for a few seconds and then he said, "How big is the load?"

"I'm not sure."

"What do you mean you're not sure? You've never asked me to assist you with your deliveries and you didn't know how much you were expecting."

"I know. But see this time it's different. I'm helping someone else bring in their product so they can set up shop," I began to explain.

Mr. Wright wasn't pleased with that answer and he made it known. "That's not a smart move on your part. You know better than to help another supplier transport his product. You're playing a very dangerous game. And I don't think I want to be a part of that."

"Come on, Mr. Wright, I need you."

"I'm sure you do," he replied and I could see the uneasiness on his face. "And believe me, I would love to take another fifty thousand dollars off your hands to finish paying for both of my daughters' college tuitions. But my gut is telling me that this one isn't right."

I instantly sat up and took heed to what he was saying, because Mr. Wright never turned me down. He had always assisted me, along with two of his most trusted LEOs. I figured if I explained to him that I knew where the dope was coming from and who the supplier was and that I had been doing business with them for some time now, then maybe he'd have a change of heart.

"Look, I know I scared you a bit when I told you I didn't know how big the load would be," I began. "But if this is any consolation, I do know who the shipment is coming from. And not only that, these guys that I am doing this for are good people. And the reason why I know this is because those same guys are the ones that supply my brother."

Mr. Wright went into think mode again. This time it took him longer than a couple of seconds. I figured now would be a good time to add icing to the cake by offering him an extra ten grand. "If you'll consider doing this for me just this time, I'll throw in an extra ten grand," I said and then I sat back and waited for him to give me his answer. I hoped he'd take the extra money as a little incentive.

While I sat there waiting on Mr. Wright to tell me what I wanted to hear, the other LEO, John entered the office carrying a white paper bag and a middle-sized cup of coffee. He smiled at me as soon as our eyes connected. "How are you Ms. Pretty Lady?" he greeted me.

I stood up from the chair because I knew I was sitting in his seat, but I also used that chance to give him a hug as well. John was an Irish cat from Long

Island. I never asked him his age but if I had to guess, I'd say he was in his mid-thirties. He wore his hair faded along the sides but spiked at the top. He sort of reminded me of the London born Soccer sensation, David Beckham. Now he wasn't as debonair, but the resemblance was strong.

After we hugged one another, I moved to the side so he could set his things down. "You didn't have to get up," he said.

"Oh, it's okay. I'm fine. Take a load off so you can eat your food," I insisted.

"Are you sure?" he pressed the issued.

"Of course I am," I said and then I stepped further to the right so I could get out of his way altogether. I wanted him to be able to get a clear view of Mr. Wright, just in case Mr. Wright wanted to bring him in on our discussion.

After several more seconds passed, I noticed Mr. Wright was fumbling around his desk like he was searching for something. I knew that wasn't a good sign. That was his way of telling me that he really didn't want to discuss the possibilities of him and his men coming on board to assist me with Miguel's shipment. But little did he know, I wasn't the type of chick that would take no for an answer.

I sighed heavily and said, "Okay, I'll tell you what, if you say yes just this one time I'll throw you an extra twenty grand instead of ten."

Mr. Wright continued to act as if he was still busy with his other workload but I saw right through it. He was playing hardball with me. And thankfully enough, John chimed in. "Oh my goodness. What did I just walk into?"

"I'm trying to get your boss over here to agree to do this job for me. But he's acting like he doesn't want to get involved," I volunteered the information to John.

"Didn't we just do a job for you?" John asked me.

"Yeah. But that was over a week and a half ago. And now I need you guys to hop on board and help me out with a shipment coming in next Tuesday morning."

"So what's the problem, Mr. Wright? Why don't you want to do it?" John asked him.

"It's more complicated than she's letting on," he finally responded.

"How is it complicated when I told you who the shipment belonged to?"

"Wait a minute, so this shipment we're talking about isn't yours?" John asked in a way as if he was seeking clarity.

"No, it belongs to the guys that supply me and my brother."

"How big is the load?" John's questions continued.

"She doesn't know," Mr. Wright interjected.

Shocked by Mr. Wright's comment, John looked like he was taken aback. And before he got a chance to question me any further, I spoke up and said, "Listen, guys, so what I don't know how big this load is supposed to be. But that doesn't mean that this job is going to be risky. We've done a lot of jobs together and they all went smoothly. Not to mention, y'all have made a great deal of money because of it. So let's look past this minor infraction and let's move forward. Time is ticking and I need an answer today."

"I will say that I'm not too crazy about the idea of not having all the specs, but considering we're not the ones who's going to be in physical contact with the load, I say let's do it," John replied and then he looked at Mr. Wright.

I couldn't help but focus my attention on Mr. Wright as well. He was John's boss, so when it was all said and done, he had the power to either give us the green light or pull the damn plug. "Come on, Mr. Wright, don't have the lady standing here all day. Just tell her yes or no," John continued.

Mr. Wright let out a long sigh and then he looked at me with the sternest expression he could muster up. I swear I had no idea what he was about to say, so I braced myself. "Aside from these business deals we do, I have had the upmost admiration for you, because you seemed like a very smart woman up until this point. Now I'm a sixth sense type of guy. I'm able to sift out shit before it even hits the fans. The only reason why I'm apprehensive about getting me and my men involved with this particular shipment is because none of us will ever know what's inside of it. Those guys you deal with could very well be dealing in firearms or explosive devices like C-4 and they will never tell you."

"Now I know you feel like you can co-sign for those guys, but I just can't take that chance. I know I'm a crooked ass federal agent who takes payoffs from people in exchange for my cooperation in allowing them to get their dope through my airport. But I will not cross the lines and turn a blind eye for two years' worth of college tuition for a couple of scum bags I don't know, who may very well have plans to blow up one of my planes. The least I can do is try to take all the precautionary measures I can so I'd be able to protect my homeland."

"So I guess the answer is no," I said quietly and meekly.

"If this was one of your shipments, I'd help you. So yes, the answer is no."

After Mr. Wright uttered the word *no,* I felt defeated. I was so devastated by the fact that he declined to help me that I couldn't see moving forward with the plans to go through with the delivery. Okay, granted, I didn't necessarily need two or three more set of eyes, but I just didn't want to take the chance of giving Evan and his crew full control of the shipment. There was always the possibility that they could throw some slick ass shit in the game by intercepting the delivery and act like it was beyond their control, so they could keep it for themselves. Now I couldn't risk that because Marco and Miguel would have me and Reggie's head.

Before I left their office, I made my final plea and hoped that they would give in. "If he'll give me clearance, I'll do it. I could definitely use the money," John said.

Trying to be optimistic, I turned my attention back to Mr. Wright. He had his back facing us, while he continued to sift through the paperwork scattered on his desk. "Will you let him do it?" I asked him.

"He won't be able to do it by himself," Mr. Wright replied.

"Well, get Rick to come in with me. I'm sure he could use the money too. He and his wife just had a baby."

"Get 'im on the radio and tell him to come to the office," Mr. Wright instructed John.

Hearing him give John the green light to assist me made me very happy. I ran over to his desk and hugged him from behind. "Thank you so much! I really appreciate you doing this for me," I told him.

"I'm sure you are. But don't come in this office and ask me or my men to assist you with this type of load again. If we're not working directly with you, then it's a no go," he warned me.

"I understand perfectly. It will not happen again," I assured him. I knew the words were a lie as soon as they left my lips.

CHAPTER 19

Backed Against the Wall

Reggie's worker, Candie, had been on my mind all day. She had been in the hospital for two days now, since her attack. I knew I wouldn't rest until I saw her, so I made it my business to stop by and see her. Visiting hours ended in fifteen minutes so I wasted very little time to get to the floor where they were housing her. When I got to the nurse's station, it only took another minute to get her room number. After I thanked the nurse that helped me, I rushed off.

Candie's room was only four doors down on the right side and the closer I got to it, the more anxious I got. Coming up here to see her was the least I could do. She was a damn good employee. She never gave Reggie and I any problems. She made sure her money was always straight. And what we liked about her most was that she was educated and loyal to a fault. Cats all over Harlem wanted her to work for them, but she would never take them on their offers, even when our supply was out and she had to wait a week to get back in the game. You could pick out all the thorough niggas from the Polo Grounds and they couldn't hold a candle to this chick.

When I entered the hospital room, I was greeted by a slew of visitors, one male and three females. The man looked like he could've been Candie's brother, because the resemblance was so strong. I surmised that the oldest woman was her mother, because of the resemblance was there as well. But the other two women didn't look like Candie at all. So I figured they were distant cousins or even her close friends.

Candie was lying in her bed wide-awake. After I spoke to everyone, including Candie, I walked over and stood alongside her bed. I tried not to stare at her face, but the cuts and bruises were somewhat unbearable to look at.

"How are you feeling?" I asked her, even though I knew it was a rhetorical question. From the condition of her face and the cast on her left arm, it was evident how she felt. I just hoped she didn't take offense to it. I was only trying to make conversation.

She tried desperately to smile. "I'm better than I was when I first came in here. Thank God for the medications they're shooting through my IV," she replied, her voice barely audible. I could tell her meds were working on her hard because she was really groggy.

"Did the doctors tell you how long you had to be in here?" I asked her.

"I believe they're gonna release her tomorrow," the older woman spoke up. "And by the way, I'm her Aunt Anna," she formally introduced herself.

I extended my hand. "Nice to me you, but I thought you were her mother."

She smiled. "She calls me her mama because I raised her from the age of six," she continued.

"Oh, how that's cool."

"This is my son Derrick, and these two are my other nieces Mona and Shelby."

I reached over and shook everyone's hand and told them that it was nice to meet them. But right when I was getting ready to turn my attention back to Candie, Aunt Anna threw a bombshell at me and started questioning me about how I knew Candie. I don't know how I did it, but lies started rolling off my tongue as if I had been prepped before I walked through the door. And what weighed in my favor was the fact that Candie was too doped up to refute anything I said.

"I know her from the neighborhood," I began to say. "My mother lives on the same floor as Candie. So when I go out there to see my mother, I'll check in on Candie to see how she and her son are doing."

"Well, you just let her neighbors know that she ain't coming back to that rat hole," Aunt Anna said. "She's going home with me."

"I don't blame you," I replied. "I would do the same."

"Would you know anything about why she was beaten up like this? Or know who could've done it?"

"I wish I did, because they wouldn't be running around in the streets right now," I answered. "Candie is a sweet person and she doesn't bother anyone. Every time I stopped by her apartment, she was either just getting in from school, cooking dinner for her son or doing homework, so she didn't deserve this at all."

"She sure didn't," her cousin Derrick, chimed in. "So as soon as I find the niggas that did this to her, I'm gonna make sure they get a room next to hers."

The fury in his tone and facial expression became very clear to me that he wanted nothing else, but to make sure her attackers felt the same pain she was feeling. At that moment, for whatever reason, I felt obligated to tell them the name of one of the guys who attacked her. But I figured if I did that, I would be put in the position to explain where I got that information from and I wasn't prepared for that. Not only that, I had just told them I didn't know who had done it. That move would have definitely created more drama for me and could possibly have gotten me entangled in his disappearance. In fact, I could picture the homicide detectives calling me to come by the precinct to answer some questions and that alone wouldn't be a good look for me. Instead of making one of the biggest mistakes of my life, I snapped back to reality and reminded myself that I needed to mind my business.

Once Candie's aunt felt like I had answered enough of her questions, she let me off the hook and kind of mellowed out a bit and allowed me to make small talk with Candie before the medication took full affect and she fell to sleep.

Before I said my goodbyes to everyone, I told Candie to call me if she needed anything. And in her sweet little voice, she assured me that she would.

On my way out of the hospital I tried to get Reggie on the line but my phone couldn't get any good reception. As soon as I got in my truck, I tried dialing his number again. This time the call went through and he answered on the third ring.

"What's up?"

"I just left the hospital from seeing Candie and she's looking pretty bad," I told him.

"Did you get a chance to talk to her?"

"Well, not really because her family was there. But she was awake so she saw me."

"When is she getting out?"

"Her aunt said she believed they were gonna discharge her tomorrow. But she ain't going back to her crib. Her aunt is taking Candie home with her."

"Well, hopefully you can get to her and find out anything else she can tell us about what happened at the Towers when she was jumped," Reggie stated.

"Don't worry. I'll come up with something," I assured him.

"Where are you on your way to now?"

"Damian and I are driving down Broadway. The big chicken was afraid to see Candie in the hospital and stayed in the car. I'm glad he did, Candie's family would have probably freaked or gotten suspicious if they saw Damian. But anyway, why did you ask?"

"Because I'm gonna need you two to make a quick stop somewhere for me," Reggie replied.

I sighed heavily because I wasn't in the mood to run one of his errands. I had just gotten off work an hour ago and came straight to the hospital to see Candie, so I was tired. Hell, I was surprised to see Damian, but Reggie was true to his word about keeping his family safe. That even meant assigning a bodyguard to Vanessa's worthless ass.

"I hope it's not far, Reggie. Shit, I'm tired and need sleep," I commented.

"Chill. I'm getting ready to hang up right now so I can text you the instructions," he told me and then disconnected the call.

Moments later, his text message came through: *Malika needs sum dough. Take her 1 grand & call me when u done.*

After I read his text and realized he wanted me to go by his pregnant baby mama's house and give her one thousand dollars, I was livid. Reggie knew I didn't walk around with that type of money on me. I would have been more upset if Damian had not had that amount of money on him. Because if he hadn't, I would have had to run to Reggie's safe house to retrieve the money and then drive back to Malika's place. I really wanted to kick Reggie's ass. But thank God for Damian for saving the day.

CHAPTER 20

The Nigga Behind the Mask

It had been a while since Sabrina and I had a chance to hang out because of everything that had been going on. Not to mention she and I had to work some strenuous flights this past week. So when she asked me if I'd go with her after work to get a bite to eat, I happily obliged. It took me damn near an hour to convince Reggie and Damian to let me have some room to myself. Damian's response was, "You have time alone when you are flying the friendly skies." I actually wanted to tell him to kiss my black ass. But I restrained and convinced them both that it had been almost five days since the attack. I could hear the pain in both of their voices, but they relented and agreed to let me hang out with Sabrina.

We were still wearing our airline uniforms and I must say, wearing them proudly. Sabrina suggested we head over to this eatery she knew in Manhattan. After the hostess seated us, she handed us our menus and told us our waiter would be with us shortly. I had to say, it was nice sitting outside in Manhattan, chilling with a friend.

While Sabrina and I chatted amongst ourselves, my Blackberry started ringing. I didn't have a man in my life and the only chick I thought was cool enough to call a friend was sitting in front of me, so I knew it had to be either Reggie, Damian or my mother calling me. I looked at the phone and the number was foreign to me. My first thought was to let it go straight to voicemail, but my curiosity overpowered that thought and I answered it before the caller could hang up.

"Hello," I said tentatively.

"So you think you're gonna keep escaping death, huh?" a creepy and scratchy voice said to me.

Alarmed by the caller's question, I immediately got the chills. My body shook and I could feel the goose bumps that had covered my body from head to toe. "Who is this?" I snapped. My intention was to get this person to continue talking with the hope that I would be able to recognize his voice. The only thing I had to go on was that the caller was a man. Other than that, my mind drew a complete blank.

"Don't worry bitch! You'll find out soon enough," my mad caller continued.

""Nah, nigga! Don't be a pussy. Stop hiding behind the phone and tell me who you are now!" I roared through my phone. I wanted an answer. I was so angry and scared at the same time I started feeling an anxiety attack coming on.

Sabrina just sat in her chair and looked at me like she was taken aback by my actions. "Who is that?" she asked me in a whisper. But I couldn't give her an answer because I didn't know myself. And being that I had gotten beside myself over this threatening call, I hadn't realized that the motherfucker hung up on me, until the busy tone started ringing in my ear. It literally scared the hell out of me.

With a look of concern, Sabrina sat up in the chair after I hung up the phone and said, "Who in the hell was that?"

Trying to process the call I had just gotten and trying to figure out what to do next was beginning to consume me. Once again, I couldn't answer Sabrina's question. But instead of allowing myself to continue to be vulnerable by sitting out in the open like I was, I shot up from my chair, took one good look at my surrounding area and then I snatched my handbag from the seat next to me and fled inside of the restaurant and walked directly to the back of the eatery. I heard Sabrina's footsteps as she ran behind me.

"Naomi, what is going on? And where are you going?" she yelled.

Once again, I couldn't get myself to answer her. The only thing I had on my mind was trying to find a way to get the fuck out of there without getting killed. And once I realized that the direction I ran in was to the restrooms, I immediately bolted inside the women's bathroom. Sabrina was right on my heels.

"Lock the door!" I instructed her. I realized that I had actually yelled at her. I was tense and afraid. *Why did I convince Damian and Reggie to give me some space? And why in the fuck didn't they overrule me?*

Sabrina locked the door and then she turned back and faced me. She looked confused but she also looked worried. "Naomi, are you going to tell me what's going on?" she pressed the issue as she walked towards me.

I hesitated for a second, trying to gather my thoughts and then I said, "A guy just called me and told me that I keep escaping death. But not too worry because he's going to find me."

Creeped out by my words, Sabrina went into panic mode. Her eyes grew five inches in diameter and then she started pacing the bathroom floor in a circle. “Oh my God! Think he called because he saw us come in here?” she asked, her voice trembling.

“I don't know. And I'm definitely not trying to find out,” I told her.

“What do you think we should do,” she asked me.

“I know I'm not leaving here.” I realized the caller had succeeded in what he probably wanted to do to me—scare the shit out of me. I had to process, but I was too damn scared.

“Call your brother. See if he can come get us.”

“He can't drive. You know he just got out of the hospital.” Fuck! I was a wreck and Sabrina was making way better suggestions than me. Thank God somebody was thinking, because my mind had suddenly gone dysfunctional.

“Call him anyway. Tell him what happened and tell him we're hiding out in the ladies bathroom and we're afraid to leave,” she explained.

Even though it had been programmed in my brain to call Reggie when tumultuous situations came up that I couldn't handle, for some odd reason it didn’t come to me. My whole state of mind had completely shut down. I believe if Sabrina wasn't with me I probably would have had a panic attack. At this very moment, I was at my wits end. I could honestly say that I was tired of living this type of lifestyle. Retiring with Damien and walking away from this operation sounded like the best solution.

When I got Reggie on the phone I gave him a brief run down about my phone call and he was not pleased to hear it. As quick thinking as Reggie was, it didn't take him no time to curse me out about not letting Damian meet me at the airport and tag along with Sabrina and I. But he told me some good news—Damian was at the house. Thank God he was at the house with Reggie and Reggie assured me that Damian would be here in a flash.

Reggie kept me on the phone. He wanted to make sure we kept a flow of communication going until Damian arrived. I knew he did this to make me feel less afraid. And it worked. He knew he was my security blanket. The sound of his voice had always put me at ease and gave me that feeling that everything would be all right.

His build and stature gave him that strong image, and money gave him power. I could honestly say that I could never remember a time when Reggie had any problems with niggas in the street. *That is, until recently.* Ninety percent of the cats that lived in Harlem had mad respect for Reggie. And since they knew that I was his baby sister, they had the same respect for me. But now the game had changed because someone wanted us eliminated. And if we didn't hurry up and find out who he or they were, then we were going to forever be looking over our shoulders. *Or worse, be six feet under.*

Finally, after waiting and talking with Reggie on the phone for seventeen minutes, Damian arrived at the restaurant. I swear I was so happy to see him. But before we excited the bathroom, he gave us very specific instructions and made us promise that we'd stick close to him and walk directly behind him until we reached our cars. And when we agreed, he led us out of the danger zone.

Chapter 21

It's Official

Damian drove as I sit in the passenger seat of my truck. I was still flustered as we left the restaurant. Damian didn't say anything when I told him I didn't want to drive or leave my whip in Manhattan. He called Reggie to tell him all was well and he was taking me home. Reggie told him he already had a car of guys on their way to Manhattan to the restaurant. One of them would return the car to Reggie's place.

I was still nervous as Damian drove. Every few seconds he would look in the rearview or side view mirrors to ensure no one was following us. He asked me for my phone, looked through the directory and called my "threatening caller" back. I heard the phone ringing and it had to ring over twenty damn times before Damian disconnected the call.

"Take me home, Damian, I don't want to go to Reggie's," I said. "I just want to get to my place, kick my shoes off and chill. I need to get some rest and I want to be alone. This stressing is fucking with me."

"There's no way I'm leaving you by yourself," Damian replied as he kept checking out the mirrors. He was calm and collected, and that should have made me feel relaxed and safe. But how could I, someone was trying to kill me. And worse, I didn't have control of my own *fucking* life, and I hated that shit.

The rest of the ride was driven in silence, and that helped to ease my mind. I had to face facts: Damian was no longer the childhood friend, I now saw him as all man and my protector.

It seemed like the time flew by fast because Damian and I approached the front door of my place in no time. After I locked the front door, I followed Damian down the hallway as he walked in every room to ensure no one was in my place. I was confident that everything would be fine, once we had a chance to settle down. Moments later, I watched him as he entered the kitchen. Before I turned the corner to enter in behind him, I heard my refrigerator door open.

"Do you ever shop for groceries?" he wondered aloud.

"Not really," I replied as I entered the kitchen.

"I can tell," he commented as he closed the refrigerator door.

I stood there near the entryway of the kitchen and watched Damian open and close every storage cabinet. "I see you got a few can goods and a couple boxes of mac and cheese," he commented.

"You wanna order out? There's this nice Thai restaurant about two blocks away from here."

"It's that the same as Chinese food?"

"No, silly, its better," I said and then I walked over and grabbed the Thai takeout menu from the kitchen drawer near the refrigerator. "I usually order their curry duck and it's good."

"Is that what you're gonna order?"

"Yep."

"Well, order me one of those too," he said as he left me standing in the kitchen by myself. I watched him from my peripheral vision. He looked and smelled like a million bucks. And the fact that he was assigned by Reggie to accompany me everywhere I went was the best decision Reggie ever made.

After I placed our order, I told Damian to listen for the door because I was going to jump in the shower. Ten minutes into my shower time, Damian knocked on the bathroom door. "Need me to wash your back?" he yelled through the door.

I stood there for a few seconds and pondered the thought of him coming in here while I was naked. Hell, washing my back actually wasn't a bad idea. I could only imagine what would happen next. I mean, it's no secret I got a nice ass. And just the thought of him smacking my ass got me hotter than the water cascading over my body. If nothing else, curiosity was killing me. I just hoped Damian could contain himself.

"Come on in," I finally told him.

In a matter of seconds, he was front and center wearing the biggest smile he could muster up. I peeped around the shower curtain, only exposing my head and gave him a suspicious look. "You looking really suspect right now," I commented.

His smile got even bigger as he approached me. "I'm just happy to be here so I can make sure no one harms you."

"Ahh . . . that's so sweet! I'm giving you two brownie points for that one," I commented sexily, but in a sarcastic fashion.

"You know me, Naomi. I'm just keeping it real."

"Yeah, I know how real you keep it, but did you come in here to talk? Or did you come in here to wash my back?"

Trying to remain cool, calm and collective, he reached out for me to hand him my washcloth. "I'm waiting on you," he said.

I handed him my washcloth after I added more liquid body wash to it and then I turned my entire body around. He slid the shower curtain to the side and it gave him complete access to my body. I moved up towards the shower nozzle so the water could run down my back a little. I also did it because I've been told that excessive amounts of water or baby oil clinging to your body makes your titties and ass look inviting. I was half Puerto Rican and Black, so you know I had an ass that gave Jennifer Lopez competition. At that very moment, Damian knew it too.

I stood with my legs spread apart, just enough to create a gap. I needed Damian to see the gap between my thighs and see how easy it would be to bend me over and get this pussy if he wanted it. Real men were indefensible and weak to gap-control, and every woman worth her weight in gold knew how to use their gap to their advantage.

"Don't be looking down at my ass!" I said and then I cracked a smile.

"Whatcha' talking about?" he replied as he scrubbed the spine of my back. "This ass," he continued as he smacked me on the butt.

With my back still facing him, I jerked my head around to look at him. "Don't start something you can't finish," I warned him.

"Oh, I can finish alright," he assured me as he continued to lather my back with the soapsuds from the washcloth.

"Yeah, okay Damian. Stay in your lane," I told him and then I turned my head back around.

Without saying another word, he dropped the washcloth on the floor of the bathtub, moved me further into the water and then he used both of his hands to wipe the suds off my entire back side. Damian's touch from his powerful hands made my pussy tingle on the inside. When he slid his hands down between my thighs and rubbed the clitoris of my pussy very slightly, it damn near sent me over the edge. It felt so good. I lifted my left leg and placed my foot on the edge of the tub so he could have better access, just in case he wanted to finger fuck me. He didn't though. Instead, he continued to play with my pussy until I started jerking and grinding it against his hand.

"Oooh, this feels so good. Please don't stop," I begged him.

"Turn around," he instructed me, in a demanding but subtle way.

I turned around to face him and before I even realized it, he pulled me towards him and planted a wet and sensual kiss on my lips. The way he sucked on my bottom lip before letting it go was passionate to say the least. He wasn't giving me too much tongue but he gave me enough. Before long he was coming out of his clothes and was completely naked. And when I say Damian gave me an eyeful, believe me. After all these years of hearing rumors of how big his dick was finally paid off. Damian's dick had to be at least eight to nine inches in length and at least two inches in diameter. And the fact that it was erect and ready to serve its purpose to make me the happiest woman in the world. It had been a while since I last had me some dick. And it had been forever since I had some good dick. So tonight I planned to ride this cat until the paint came off the wall.

"I want you to give me that dick from the back," I whispered into his ear while I was kissing him around his neck.

"Nah, I want you to get on this dick and ride it," he told me. "I wanna look in your eyes while I'm holding you in my arms."

Shocked but turned on at the same time that he was so open and honest with his feelings that my feelings for him grew more and more by the second. I couldn't decipher whether or not it was lust or something else. I did know that whatever it was, I didn't want the feeling to stop. While I had my legs harnessed around his waist tightly, he held a firm grip around both of my ass cheeks as I slid his hard dick inside of me. I gasped, as I tighten my vagina muscles and grabbed him tightly around his neck.

"Ouch. Wait. Wait," I said.

"Just relax baby. I gotcha," Damian said, while I began to feel him maneuver by pushing himself slowing inside of me. Damn, of course he knew how to maneuver that slab of meat between his legs.

I loosened my grip around his neck and tried to relax a little more. The feeling of him inside of me was a bittersweet moment. The girth and length of his manhood hurt, but when he started pushing himself back and forth inside of me in slow motions, it started feeling good. In fact, I started grinding my pussy against his dick so I could create some wet friction between us. Thank God I was a perfect weigh and frame for him. The way he was gyrating and pumping his dick inside of me while he cupped my ass in the palm of his hands sent chills down my spine.

Damian was handling his fucking business.

I knew if I were any bigger, then he wouldn't be handling me the way he's doing. The more he pushed himself in me, the harder I grinded my pussy against his dick. The heat from the shower water penetrated my back the way Damian was penetrating my pussy. The pounding and the constant friction from both of us felt incredible.

"Your pussy feels so good, I don't even wanna come. I could keep my dick inside you all night long," he told me.

His words made my heart flutter. Sparks were jumping around my heart like fireworks. I lifted my head up from his neck and pulled his face to mine and began giving him, long passionate kisses. I felt where he was coming from because I didn't want him to stop either. But they say all good things come to an end, and they were right, because while we were kissing, he started penetrating me with shorter and harder pumps. I knew his dick was about to burst, so I stopped kissing him and whispered into his ear. "If you really want me to be your wife, don't take it out. I'll give you a baby," I told him and then I tightened my legs around his waist really tight. I wanted him to know that I was for real. And when he tightened his grip around my ass, I knew then that he wanted the same thing. "Give me that dick. Fuck me harder! And don't stop," I moaned, while I continued to throw my pussy back at him.

Without a moment's notice, his grip on me got even tighter. Then his knees started buckling. I thought at one point that he might drop me because his facial expression looked like he was about to have a fucking seizure. Then when he turned me around and pressed my back against the wall of the shower to take some of my weight off him, he shot his juices in me like it was the fourth of July. I'm sure most of it went inside of me, but the rest dripped down my thighs as soon as he pulled himself out of me.

Damian looked exhausted, so I pushed him back from me so I could stand on my own two feet. And when I was able to stand up on my own, I threw my arms back around him and looked into his eyes. "You feel better?" I asked him.

He smiled. "Never better."

"Well, since you did all the work. Let me wash you up so you can get out of here before our food gets here."

"Sounds like a plan."

It didn't take me long to bathe him nor myself. When I was done, I got out of the shower a few minutes after he left. I found him standing in the middle of my living room floor drying himself off and then he put his boxing shorts back on. I headed to my bedroom so I could put on one of my many pieces of sleepwear. While I was spraying one of my favorite perfumes around my neck, Damian snuck up behind me and embraced me from behind. He startled me. "You scared the crap out of me," I whined and then I tried to hit him in his arm but he wouldn't let me move.

"Stop trying to fight this love I got for you," he commented.

We were standing in front of my bedroom mirror looking at one another through the reflection while he held onto me from behind. I tried to drop my head so he couldn't see my expression, but as soon as I tried to lower my head, he lifted it back up with his hand.

"Why do you keep fighting me? You know I can love you the way you need to be loved," he continued.

"I'm not fighting you."

"Then what is it? I've been trying to be with you for the longest. But you kept giving me the cold shoulder."

"I just didn't want to go there with you."

"Why not?"

"Damian, I've known you for a very long time, I've seen the women you've been with. And there were lots of them."

"They didn't mean shit to me. You are the woman I always wanted," he said and then he kissed me on my neck. "Right now, I can honestly say that I am the happiest man on the face of this earth."

I tried to say something but my mouth wouldn't open. I was feeling the sparks coming from my heart. I didn't want to admit it, but he did make me feel good.

"Did you really mean when you said that you'd give me a baby as long as I made you my wife?"

I wanted to say *yes*. But again, my mouth wouldn't open. I did manage to nod my head though. And when I did that, he said, "Well, when all of this shit is over with, we're gonna go by my jeweler so we can pick you out the most flawless, five-carat, cushion cut diamond ring they have."

"You sure you're ready for all of that?"

"I was ready for this day a long time ago."

"Have you thought about what Reggie is going to say, when you tell him about us?"

"No, not really. But we'll see."

"Yep, you're definitely right about that," I said.

Twenty minutes later, we got our food delivered. Damian and I sat down on the sofa in my living room and tore into our food like we were starving. We made small talk in between bites. When he wasn't looking, I watched the way he ate his food. I couldn't help but picture the man who would be living with me. He seemed like he would be okay. But good dick had a way of clouding a woman's judgment, so I convinced myself to slow my roll before I gave this nigga too much credit. I knew I had to slow walk this relationship just to see if he was really on the up and up with me. I had fucked a slew of niggas in my time and over half of them were full of shit. The rest of them were cool but they had other issues like baby mamas or they couldn't stay out of jail, so they had to go. I just hoped that Damian would be different.

Chapter 22

One Plus One Equals Bullshit

After what I experienced last night with the threatening phone call and Damian and I hooking up, all I wanted to do was lie in the bed since I didn't have to go to work. But unfortunately that idea came to a halt when Reggie started ringing my phone off the hook.

"Hello," I said, sounding all groggy.

"You still sleep?" he asked.

"Yeah."

"Where is Damian? Put him on the phone," he instructed me.

"Alright," I said and then I pretended to act as if I was moving around. Then I put my phone on mute so he wouldn't hear me waking Damian up. It took two shoves and a pat on his back to get him to open his eyes.

"What's up?" he asked, his voice barely audible.

"Reggie wants to talk to you," I told him and before I handed it to him, I took it back off mute.

"Hello," Damian said and then he waited for Reggie to respond. I sat up in the bed and tried to eavesdrop on their conversation, but I couldn't hear exactly what Reggie was saying. I heard his voice, but I couldn't make out what he was saying.

About ten seconds later, Damian said, "A'ight. Well, give me about an hour and we'll be over there."

Once he ended the call, he handed the phone back to me and then he laid his head back against the pillow. He closed his eyes and acted like he was about to go back to sleep. So I nudged him and asked him what did Reggie say?

"He told me he wanted us to have a meeting and to meet him at the hideout spot."

"Was that it?"

"Yeah, basically."

"So when you plan to leave?"

"I'ma lay right here for another thirty minutes, but you can go ahead and get dressed if you want to."

I let out a long sigh because in all honesty, I did not feel like leaving out of the damn house this early. I was trying to sleep in for a little while, but Reggie's cock blocking ass had to call and fuck that one up.

I slid out of the bed and took a quick shower since I had bathed the night before. When I got out the shower, I slipped on pair of all-white capris and an all-white Marc Jacob V-neck t-shirt with the MC initials in the center. By the time I had gotten completely dressed, Damian was up and had gotten dressed, so we left soon there- after.

En route to our hideaway apartment across town, I got a call from Sabrina wanting to know if I was okay. I really wasn't comfortable with her in my business for fear that she'd draw her own conclusions, so I downplayed the entire event.

"Are you sure you're okay?" she asked again.

"Yes, I'm fine," I lied.

"Are you sure because what happened last night was really scary. I worried about you all last night long."

"I'm fine really. I just overreacted. But I'm better."

"Having some guy call and threaten that he's going to kill you, Naomi, isn't overreacting. I think you should call the police, at least, so you can have it on file," she pressed the issue.

"Are you working today?" I asked, trying to change the subject.

"Yeah, I'm here now, sitting in the lounge area," she told me.

"Who's in there with you?"

"Nobody but me and Tracy. Evelyn just left out a few minutes ago. They got her flying on another flight. Oh yeah, she just asked about you too. Wanted to know what you were doing on your time off? And I told her after what happened to you last night, you'll probably be better off at work around a whole bunch of security."

I swear my fucking blood pressure shot sky high listening to this dumb ass chick on the other end of the line. She was my best girl friend and I knew she meant well, but at times she could stick her nose where it wasn't wanted at times. And the fact that she was at work talking about me really made me livid. I could hear her now, giving that bitch, Evelyn, every single detail about what transpired last night, throwing up red flags that I might be into some shit that I didn't need to be in. I knew if I was standing in front of Sabrina at this very moment, I would've smacked the fuck out of her and dared the bitch to hit me back.

"Sabrina, I can't believe you opened up your mouth and told Evelyn my motherfucking business like that. That bitch ain't my friend for real. She pretends to be, but she ain't. So why did you feed into her larceny? She's a fraud and you fell right into her trap."

"I'm sorry, Naomi, I didn't see it like that," she began to explain.

"Come on now, Sabrina, you know better than that."

"I know. I know. But she just sounded so sincere."

"That's what phony ass people do," I spat. I was angry that Sabina would just spill her fucking guts just like that. That bitch had never hung out with us before, but she tried to carry it like she's down with us. She just started working at the airline with us a couple of months ago, so she hadn't been around long. "So what exactly did you tell her?"

"I just told her about the phone call you got from that guy and that you had gotten pretty shaken up about it."

"That grimy ass bitch! I swear I wanna call her nosy ass so bad right now and give her a piece of my mind," I barked.

While I was fuming at the mouth and going off on the phone, I noticed the way Damian was looking at me. He didn't interrupt my conversation, but he looked as if he was concerned about me.

"Naomi, I am so sorry. She acted like she was all concerned, that's why I told her," Sabrina continued to explain and I was getting a really bad taste in my mouth the longer I stayed on the phone with her ass. Instead of cursing her silly ass out, I advised her to keep her mouth closed from this day forward. I didn't care who asked about me at work, because at the end of the day, they didn't mean shit to me.

"Naomi, I promise that will never happen again," she assured me.

"Yeah, alright," I said and then I hung up without saying goodbye.

I threw my Blackberry inside of my handbag and laid my head back against the passenger headrest of my truck. I tried to calm myself down, but I was finding that very hard to do. Damian reached over and placed his right hand on my thigh and told me to breathe slowly. But I couldn't do it. I wanted to vent. No, I need to vent. Then I would be able to calm down and breathe slowly.

"Do you know that dumb ass girl went to our coworker and told her about that phone call I got last night?"

"I heard you."

"Wasn't that the dumbest thing she could've done? I mean, what possessed her to do that? She's from the streets just like we are. So she knows when and when not to open her fucking mouth."

"Maybe she did it because she felt like she was helping you," Damian replied.

"Well, if she thought she was helping me out by doing that crazy shit, then I'll hate to see what she'll do to fuck me over," I replied sarcastically and then I turned my attention to the people we passed by in the streets. Maybe I was overreacting. Sabrina didn't know what I was doing on the side and she was my friend, maybe she did think she was actually helping me.

Damian continued to massage my thigh. I had to admit, his strong hand felt good on my skin. He wasn't trying to be there, he was here . . . and just that thought should have put me on C square—cool and calm. But I couldn't, or wouldn't, allow myself to chill.

"It's gonna be alright," Damian said.

"Oh, I know it is because I'm putting her ass on ice. The only time she's gonna see and talk to me is when I'm at work," I replied and then drifted off and imagined what went through Evelyn's mind when Sabrina told her what really happened. I could picture her now, trying to figure out what I had going on in my life. I was sure she would give away her entire paycheck to get the goods about my lifestyle. All of them were nosy bitches and if they kept it up, I was going to give them something to really talk about.

Just as I was about to relax and spend the rest of the ride in complete silence, my phone rang again. I looked at the number and didn't recognize it. And this point, I wasn't answering another call whereas I didn't recognize the number. I wasn't going through what I went through at the restaurant.

Damian sensed my hesitation and took the phone from me. He looked at the number, and then answered, "What?" He listened for all of ten seconds before handing the phone back to me. "It's Candie, she says she needs to talk to you . . . sounds important."

"Candie, I'm glad you are out the hospital," I said immediately after I took the phone from his hand and pressing the speaker button.

"Thank you, Naomi for coming by the hospital to see me." The sound of her voice put a smile on my face and made me feel kind of good. "My family was happy I had one friend who cared about me. You were the only one who came to see me and I really appreciate that."

"It wasn't a problem, it was my pleasure," I replied. "So, what's up?"

"Well," she said, and then she fell silent. I noticed the tone in Candie's voice changed. "What's going on Candie? Are you alright?"

"I was talking to Angel—"

"You talking about the chick with the one arm who used to work for my brother?" I interrupted Candie.

"Yes. Angel and I kinda grew up together. We went to the same middle and high school, and have always been cool with each other." Candie pause for several seconds. But actually it seemed as if it was several minutes than seconds. She had piqued my interest and I wanted to know what was going on. I liked Candie but I wasn't interested in hearing anything about Angel.

"Well, Angel was afraid to tell you the day she saw you getting on the elevator that she knew you were about to be set up. She said she overheard Ben and Dre talking about it the night before the whole shit went down."

"What?" I said. I was on edge. My heart started racing. "You mean to tell me that those motherfuckers set me up to get robbed?" I snapped.

"Yep. And she said she also heard Dre telling Ben that he couldn't wait before they took over y'all whole operation. And with the young assassins on their team it wouldn't be long before it happens."

"What? That's bullshit, Candie. Don't buy into that shit. I don't know what kind of stunt that bitch Angel, is trying to pull, but I ain't going to feed into it. She's trying to start an unnecessary war within our camp because of what happened to her and her brother. Dre and Ben would never betray Reggie. Reggie has been too good to those niggas for them to act like that."

At that statement, Damian swirled through traffic and pulled to the side of the road. He took my phone.

"Candie, when did Angel tell you this?" Damian asked.

"She told me the night I was beat up and got sent to the hospital. As a matter of fact, they beat her up too. But I don't know what they did with her. A lot of people are saying she's missing. That's why I can't go back home. I'm afraid they might try to get rid of me too."

"Fuck," Damian said. I looked at his face and I could tell he believed every word Candie said. I was stunned. Not Dre and Ben. They were good soldiers. They wouldn't do this to Reggie. This was too fucking unbelievable.

"Thanks, Candie. Now lay low and I'm gonna make sure you are taken care of."

I was still stunned and couldn't believe my ears. What the fuck was going on?

"Thanks, Damian, but it wasn't about that. You, Reggie and especially Naomi, have been good to me and always treated me right. I just wanted to return the gesture."

"Still, we are going to take care of you," Damian replied.

"Damian, that's not all. About an hour or so before Angel and I were attacked, I saw Reggie's wife, Vanessa, leaving out of my building."

"Are you sure it was Vanessa?" Damian shouted loudly.

"I know exactly how she looks. It was Vanessa because when she left, I watched her get into Reggie's black Suburban."

"Oh shit! She ain't lying. Vanessa was driving Reggie's truck because that was around the time he was in the hospital." I pointed out to Damian.

"Yep, you're right." Damian agreed.

"Was there anyone with her?" I yelled out loud, hoping she could answer me.

"Yeah," Candie stated. As much as I liked Candie and was happy she was telling us this, especially if this was true, I really didn't want to hear anything else. "She went out the side door that no one uses. I saw Dre at the door and he hit her on the ass as she walked out the door. She turned around and acted like she didn't like it, but when she turned back around, she had a smile on her face."

"Are you fucking kidding me? This bitch is playing my fucking brother behind some block hustling ass nigga! How dare that bitch!"

"Yo' Candie, please tell us you're playing a joke on us." Damian said.

"No, I'm not joking at all. I almost died at the hands of those niggas. And now that I'm still alive, and know what I know about them, it's time to give them what they got coming to them."

"Oh my God! Reggie isn't going to take this shit very well. He is going to go on a rampage." I commented.

"Yeah, and Vanessa's head is going to be the first on the chopping block. He ought to beat her ass, put her out and make her move in Candie's old spot since she wants to hang out there."

"Not after I spit in the bitch's face first!" I spat.

Damian and I looked at each other. It would be another two minutes before he put the truck in drive.

CHAPTER 22

What's Done in the Dark

Reggie was already at our hideaway spot by the time we arrived. I rushed in the apartment to tell him what was going on. He must have heard us coming because he opened the door right before I reached it. Damian was lagging behind me. I guess he was going to let me break the bad news by myself. I was about to open my mouth when Reggie put his finger over his lips signaling me to be quiet. He was on the phone talking to someone. I tried to break into his conversation and he was giving his best *chill out* face. I was anxious and I suspected that phone call wasn't as important as the information I had to tell him. I returned his looks with my own looks of anxiousness and importance, and he blew me off.

By that time, Damian had come through the door and I said fuck it and got me a bottle of water from the refrigerator in the kitchen and went into the TV room where everyone else was and took a seat next to Reggie. He still wore his bandages, but he was recovering well to say the least. I sat there quietly and waited for him to end his call.

Although Reggie looked good, I was surprised he was driving. I hadn't seen him in two days, but he had told me only yesterday that he wouldn't be driving for several more days. I guess he said the hell with it since he didn't want anyone else to know about this place, but Damian and me.

When he finally got off the phone, I asked the question, "I thought you weren't driving for a few more days?"

"I'm not," he answered matter-of-factly. Both Damian and I looked at him as if he was taking too many drugs.

"How did you get here?" Damian asked, I was sure out of curiosity.

"I drove him here," Stone surprised us. I didn't know how old Stone was exactly, but I was sure he wasn't quite sixty yet. But he still looked good, for an older guy. He stood about six feet four or six five, and was lean as a twenty-five year old athlete. He looked powerful and distinguished at the same time. His hair was chopped very close, the shadow look, not bald but the closest you could get to being bald, and his mustache attached to his well-groomed, neatly trimmed beard, which also connected to his thin sideburns. I had never thought of Stone in the sexual sense, but damn, he looked better than the old motherfuckers I slept with.

"So what's going on?" I asked as I sat in one chair, while Stone signaled Reggie to sit at the computer near the entrance of the TV room. Damian took the other chair while Stone stood.

"You tell us," Reggie chimed in.

I told Reggie and Stone about the conversation Damian and I had with Candie. I made sure I didn't leave out anything. I looked at Damian as I tried to repeat Candie's words as best as I could. And after I delivered my big news, I noticed that the expressions on the men faces were stoic. They could have been guards at Buckingham Palace with those damn faces. And the fact that I couldn't make light of it, I sat there and waited for someone to say something.

"Damn, it's beginning to make sense," Reggie said.

"What is?" Damian asked.

"Scotty was shot in the head this morning when he was taking Vanessa over her mother's house . . . and supposedly, she was kidnapped. Those young niggas from that crew took credit for the kidnapping. Supposedly it was payback for us killing Lil' Man, the cat that was with him and the two cats at the mall. They are asking for one million dollars for her worthless ass. But now that I know she's behind this shit, she needs to keep her dumbass right where she is. Because if I ever get a chance to see her, I know I'm gonna break her fucking neck with my bare hands."

"That trifling bitch!" I spewed. I could feel the venom and hatred in my heart for that snake of a woman. She was a lowlife, ass worm. And I felt bad for insulting worms like that.

"Calm down," Damian said to me.

"No, fuck that! I think we—"

"Shut up, Naomi," Reggie interrupted me. "Damian is right, you need to calm down. Let me be the irrational nigga around here. Not you. It ain't in your nature. Right now, we are here for a reason. All of this information was right on time and it was what we needed to know. Stone called us here and he needs to share his information as well."

We all turned our attention to Stone. He was the cool one. The one who was just taking in everything—as only Stone could do.

"Before we watch the video I have for you guys, let me tell you that I managed to have a one-on-one conversation with your friend, Walt, and a one-on-four session with members of those gang members."

Stone hesitated. I know it was his way of letting us digest what he was saying and about to say.

"Walt told me Vanessa had put a hit out on your parents," Stone continued.

I immediately looked at Reggie and noticed that he wasn't too happy about what Stone had just said. I could see the veins in his neck popping. Our mother and Foxx were our life. And the last thing we wanted to do was put our mother's life in jeopardy. Foxx had been around the block a time or two so he knew how to take care of himself. But our mother was innocent. Instead of being in Philly, she should be chilling in her home back here in New York.

"Don't worry, I took care of business," Stone reassured us. "They are still in Philly, at the same house. And yes, they are safe. Evidently, the young assassins aren't that smart. The leader of the group gave three of the young assassins the address: 4897 Clarendon Street."

I smiled when Stone said the address. Foxx and Mom were at 4798 Clarendon Place. If you were unfamiliar with Philly, there is a Clarendon Place, Clarendon Lane and Clarendon Street. But they were all in different neighborhoods. I also noticed Stone and Reggie smiling as well.

"Well, you know that was the wrong address," Stone said, still smiling. "Needless to say, as luck would have it, the address the three so-called assassins went to was the brownstone of one of Philadelphia's finest—a cop. He noticed when the kids drove up and got out of their car, with their burners in hand and sky masks covering their faces."

This shit was unbelievable. Who in the fuck did these young kids think they were the fucking Bloods or the Crips? Damn, they were asking to be killed.

"The cop came outside with his pistol in hand and ordered them to stop and put their weapons down but they bucked on him. And within seconds a shootout came underway and those three cats were gunned down."

"Unbelievable! Those little niggas had plenty of heart, huh?"

No one responded to my comment, which I really didn't expect anyone to respond. But this was crazy.

"Now, before I go any further. I gotta let you know that your parents are safe and sound. And you guys don't need to worry about them." Stone continued.

"How we know that bitch, Vanessa, ain't going to send another army of niggas out to look for them?" I asked frantically. "She's such a fucking snake that she might even go out looking for them herself and then after she finds them, she makes her call for someone to come and put a slug in their head while she's standing right there with them. I swear I don't put shit past her anymore."

"No need to worry about all of that. Trust me, this situation is under control," Stone stated. "Let me start the video. But before I do, this is pretty gruesome stuff, Naomi. You sure you want to view this?"

Coming from anyone else, I would have been upset. But Stone wasn't anyone else. He really was more of an uncle to Reggie and me than our own uncles. He cared about us. But I was knee deep in this business and now it was personal since my bitch of a sister-in-law had brought Foxx and Mom into this mess.

I didn't say anything. And Stone took that as a nod of agreement on my part. He stepped in front of Reggie at the computer; hit the space key and the computer came to life from its sleep mode. Then Stone put in a thumb drive, hit several keys and the video fired up.

On the twenty-seven inch computer monitor that also served as a TV was three teenagers tied to a chair in a basement. As I looked at the monitor, I realized it wasn't just any basement. It was the basement of Reggie's computer store. Additionally, I noticed the kids' faces were completely covered in blood from a thorough ass kicking by someone. That someone was probably Stone.

Stone turned up the computer speakers and the first thing we heard was, "I commend the three of you for taking a beat down like grown men, but now comes the fun stuff."

It was Stone's voice. As bad as I hated these three kids, I felt kind of bad for them. They were no match for Stone.

"Now one of you three are gonna tell me what I want to know. And whoever that person is, he may actually get a chance to see his twenty-first birthday one day."

Then Stone threw a couple of pails of water in the three boys' faces. All three were awake, but their eyes were closed or damn near closed. Two of the boys had their shirts removed. The third had a light color shirt, which was soaked in blood, and now, water. And they were truly boys. They had to be maybe sixteen or seventeen. No more than eighteen.

"You guys are without a leader, without a gang now," Stone continued his fear tactics on the boys. "Your three homeboys that went to Philly are dead. And four more of your people got killed the other day. I actually liked the way the one died." Stone began to chuckle. "You know, being thrown from a building while you're tied up in a chair is a quick and easy way to die. All I would have to do is pick each one of you up, one at a time and toss you over the ledge. It would be nothing for me. So, tell me who wants to go first? Unless somebody feels like they'll be more beneficial staying alive. And if that's the case then you're gonna have to start talking now"

I turned my head and noticed Stone wasn't saying anything, just taking in the video like the rest of us. The scary part about the video was the pitch and tone of his voice. His size was already an intimidation factor, but just the way he spoke. He was calm and deliberate, like he was the executioner about to pull the switch on a person about to die on death row.

The kid in the middle seat raised his head. His right eye was almost completely open. We could see his eyeball and the redness of his eye. His left eye was damn near closed but not as bad as the other two boys. Something told me Stone planned it that way. But the boy had a look of doubt after Stone's statement about their boss.

"Oh, you don't believe me," Stone said on the video. "Well, let me give you something from your boss."

Then the most unbelievable thing happened. All three of the boys started screaming and yelping as Stone was putting something on them. As I looked closer, I really couldn't believe my eyes. Stone tossed severed body parts on the three boys. The boys started losing it, because Stone actually shoved the dismembered hands and cut off ears into their mouths. The sight of the guys being forced fed body parts made me sick to my stomach. I ran as fast as I could to the bathroom and I threw up in the toilet. I heard Damian say stop the video. And I can only assume Reggie did, because the boys in the video stopped screaming. Or, at least, their screams were on pause.

"You okay," Damian asked me as he turned on the water and grabbed a face towel off the towel rack.

"Yeah," I managed to say. "That was fucked up. Making those boys eat a dead person's ears. Come on, Damian, what kind of shit is that?"

"That's the kind of shit we deal with, Naomi," Damian replied as he put the cold face cloth on the nape of my neck. After holding it there for some seconds and us not saying anything, he removed the face towel from my neck and helped me off the floor. Then he told me to wash my face as he open the cabinet and opened the bottle of mouthwash.

After I rinsed my mouth out, I looked at him. I wanted to kiss him so badly as well as wrap my arms around him. But this wasn't the time or place. I could tell he wanted the same. But Reggie didn't know yet and this was not the time to inform him of Damian and I. So Damian grabbed me by the hand and led me back to the bedroom.

When we got to the room, Stone said, "Naomi, if you want to listen to the rest of this, you can do that outside the door, you don't have to watch the rest of the video."

"No, I'm fine, Uncle Stone," I lied. With that, Reggie hit the pause button and the video continued.

"You sick, old man," the boy in the middle chair said. I assumed he was the leader of this band of the gang members there. Better yet, ex-assassins. "I don't know all dem' niggas you talking about but I do know that a nigga named Kay-B who was supposed to get paid to kidnap Reggie's wife but make it look like a real kidnapping. And his wife is da' one who hired us."

"That's all I wanted to know," Stone said on the video.

"What you gonna do wit' us, man? You gonna let me live, right? I told you everything I knew."

Then the video went black.

I didn't ask any questions. Nor did anyone else.

"By the way," Stone said to Reggie, Damian and me, "the leader of the Assassins for Hire wasn't Walt. He was their fall guy."

"Well who's body parts did they belong to?" I somehow managed to say without a problem.

Stone looked at me, stepped towards me and gave me a peck on the forehead. The same thing he would do after he let Reggie and me stay up late watching scary movies, and then he would tuck me in bed. And he always managed to do one thing—give me a kiss on the forehead. That meant I wasn't getting an answer. I hated when I was left in the dark about shit.

CHAPTER 23

D - Day

Today was the day of the first shipment for Miguel. I was tired but surprisingly I wasn't nervous. In my mind, I didn't have anything to be nervous about. I figured it was because I felt secure and safe when I was doing my job. All of the madness stayed back in New York.

This was a long day for me and the crew. Our flight was taking off at six thirty that morning. First, we were flying to Phoenix, followed by a two-hour layover. Then we were flying to Dallas, followed by another hour and a half layover. Then the flight crew was changing. Our regular crew would stay the night and take the first flight to New York the next day. We flight attendants always flew back to New York that same day, but not as part of the crew. We helped out if the new crew needed help, but we were tag-a-longs. The airline started doing this after 9/11, but went back to the regular schedule around 2007. Then the recession hit and the airline went back to this same old crazy schedule.

Ironically, I loved it. It helped me when it came to planning and scheduling shipments for Reggie and I. And I knew the long layovers in Phoenix and Dallas were to ensure all of the corporations' packages that were packed on the plane.

When I was in Dallas, I got a chance to talk to Damian. He had me call an unknown number on one of the pay phones in the Dallas airport.

"Hey you, I miss you already," Damian said.

Although it brought a smile to my face, I wanted to play it cool. "Really, what do you miss about me?" I replied.

"Check you out," Damian responded. "I love it when you play hard to get. But remember you're gonna pay for it when you get back here." I heard him laughing when he said that.

I had to laugh too when I heard Damian laugh. "I'm looking forward to it."

"Talk to Reggie yet?"

"Briefly. I swear I was about to tell him about us this morning. But then I chickened out. I was afraid of how he would react," I replied. Quite frankly, neither one of us knew how he would feel about our new status. And I actually think Damian was just as afraid as I was, but he was too damn hood to say it out loud.

"I understand. So, if this will make you feel any better just take your time because with everything that's going on, now is not the right time anyway," Damian said. "Speaking of which, I need to let you know what's going on."

Those words immediately piqued my interest. "Well, what are you waiting on, tell me what's up," I demanded.

"Well, as you know we agreed not to let Dre and Ben know that we knew what was going on. But somehow they picked up on something because we got a call that they're wilding out around there. Dre is starting beef with a few of the niggas in the other buildings."

"Did they say why?"

"Since we got the plug about what he and Ben were trying to do, we shut down the whole shop. Nobody out there has any of our stuff. It's like a ghost town and those niggas are going crazy because they don't have any work."

"They never acted like that before when we ran out."

"Exactly. Which is why we really know what time it is with them niggas. Any other time they wouldn't be getting all crazy, but the reason why they're doing it now is because they know we still got plenty of product left. And the fact that we're telling them differently is getting them cats on the edge. We're stopping their flow and their plans to fuck up our operation and they ain't like that this too much."

"How long do y'all plan to do this?"

"Until we find Vanessa. Unfortunately, she's gone into deep hiding. Her mother, sisters and brother aren't answering their phones and all have left their houses. But we have someone at each of their homes in case they come back."

"What does Reggie plan to do in the meantime?"

"Concerning Vanessa?"

"Yeah,"

"Well, he just closed all of the accounts and credit cards they had together, and thanks to Stone, he was even able to empty out the bank accounts in her name alone. And don't ask me how your uncle did that. That nigga got connections all over the fucking place."

I laughed at Damian's remark. But he was right, Stone was a well-connected guy.

"And lastly, we haven't been able to get any information on the last two assassins. We think they are chilling with Dre, Ben and Vanessa. But Reggie is cool. His mind is focused. I went with him to his physical therapy today and he looked good. I think all of this shit had him motivated to get back into the action. As soon as we left physical therapy, we went to the field where we do our target practice, and he shot off at least fifty rounds."

"I just hope he finds that trifling bitch and make her pay for all the shit she's put him through," I said.

"Don't worry. Her day will come." Damian said.

"Well, I hope so. She's been walking around for far too long especially with all the shit she's done."

"Be patient baby. Be patient. Everything is going to happen when it's supposed to. It's all about timing."

Damian was right. Timing was a key factor. A lot of people fuck up and get themselves in shit they can't get out of because they react out of emotions. Women do it all the time, which is why we can't run the fucking world. At the end of the day, I wanted to hear that Vanessa's ass was tortured and that we didn't have to worry about her grimy ass anymore. I mean how dare that bitch put out a hit on my parents? They've never done shit to her cold-hearted ass. Reggie was the one who fucked around on her, not my parents. So, it was just a matter of time before karma catches up with her.

Although it was a long day, I was happy when the plane landed in New York a good twenty minutes early. I was more ecstatic that we could pull right in the gate. Usually when we landed early, especially this early, there was always another plane in our assigned gate, usually waiting to take off. But not this time.

Since this wasn't an overnight trip, I just had my overnight handbag. I usually waited on Sabrina, but I was still upset with her after I found out she told that bitch all my business, so I grabbed my things from the overhead compartment and turned my phone on and saw I had a ton of voicemail messages that had come in during my three hour flight from Dallas.

I called my voicemail and the first message was a frantic message from Damian. "Naomi, somebody blew the whistle! The Feds raided the Polo Grounds and tried to raid Reggie's penthouse, but Reggie was able to get away. Be careful and call me as soon as you get this message."

What the fuck! I was nervous now. I didn't understand what was going on.

I listened to the next message. This one was from Mr. Wright. "Naomi, we have a problem. The DEA and FBI both called and plan on intercepting your flight as soon as it lands. What I'm told is both agencies received an anonymous phone call from someone who told the Feds that you and your brother are running a drug smuggling operation through our airlines. They had a lot of questions for me and my boys. They know someone is working with you guys, they just don't know who it is. If you get this message in time, I had Rick to pull out his old Halloween costume from last year that he has stored away in his locker. It's an old woman's wig, a dress and some makeup left for you inside of the waste basket on the side wall of the last stall of the second restroom departing your gate. You know the one—"

Fuck, the message cut off. I hit the next message and Mr. Wright completed his voicemail message. "Okay, your phone cut me off. It's the last stall in the second restroom. You know which one I'm talking about, we have talked about this before. There will be an Out of Order sign on the stall door. If you don't get this message in time and the Feds get a hold of you, please don't panic. The Feds have nothing. It's the corporations' shipments and most judges, even Federal judges, will not give them a search warrant that easily based on the word of an anonymous phone call. That shit never happens." he continued and then the message cut off again.

Fuck! My nerves were all over the place. After all the passengers exited the plane I stood there not knowing whether or not it would be safe to leave the aircraft myself. Thoughts of Federal Agents bailing towards me while I attempted to make my escape became overwhelming and scary. My heart raced uncontrollably. I had no idea what to do. I did know that whatever I decided to do, I needed to do it very quickly because there would be a cleanup crew coming aboard this aircraft at any second. Meanwhile I managed to clear my mind long enough to get Damian on the phone. He sounded like he was in complete distress. "Had your flight landed yet? Where are you?"

"Everybody left the plane but I'm still on board trying to figure out what to do. I got the message about the Feds going up in the spot at the Polo Grounds and Reggie's house."

"Look baby girl, get off that plane now. And get out of that airport as soon as you can without getting spotted." his instructions began.

"And go where? I heard that the Feds are all over the fucking place looking for us."

"Try to get back to the spot where you and Reggie got your emergency travel bag and I'll meet you there."

"What time are you going to be there?" I panicked. I didn't want anything to happen to him. He and I had already planned to spend the rest of our life together so we can't start it off like this. I couldn't picture him going to jail. Or even I for that matter. I knew we needed to be very careful about how we went about this thing.

"I'll be there when I can."

"How long do you want me to wait for you?"

"If I'm not there within the hour than leave and go south."

"Go down south where? I don't know anyone who lives down south."

"Listen to me Naomi, you're gonna have to calm down. Let's just take this thing one step at a time and meet me at the spot. Hopefully, I'll be able to finally get in touch with Reggie before I meet up with you."

"Think I got enough time to go and clean out my place before they get there?"

"I'm not sure. But, you can try. Just be careful though."

"Alright." I said and then I ended our call.

After I got up the gumption to exit the plane, I inconspicuously made my way by all the hundreds of passengers and into the ladies restroom that Mr. Wright had instructed me to go to. As soon as I entered into the stall, I grabbed the contents from the waste basket and immediately got dressed. When I was done, I walked out of the stall and looked myself in the mirror. I couldn't help but smile because I swear I didn't recognize myself with this grayish colored wig with streaks of black, an old faded blue dress, a pair of orthopedic shoes and a folded-up walking cane. And once I finished taking inventory of myself, all I had to do was unfold the walking cane.

I knew I should've left my handbag behind and stashed it inside of the wastebasket but I needed it. I had too much valuable shit with me to carry in my hands, so I pressed forward. Now all I needed to do was get out of the airport before the Feds made it here. The bad part was I had to act the part of an older lady and walk with a cane while carrying a one thousand dollar overnight handbag. Now was the moment of truth.

Everything was going well. I had made ground by getting to the nearest exit but right after I walked by the baggage pickup area, I immediately noticed several Federal Agents who were being accompanied by the airport police and I damn near had a heart attack. They were fifty feet away from me and if I wanted to make my escape, then now was the perfect time. Unfortunately for me, every government agent with a badge and gun had every exit in this entire fucking airport blocked off. I was pissed at myself because I had to move slower than I wanted to. I probably played the part of the old, crippled woman too good. Time was of the essence and I had picked up my walk, but I didn't want to overdo it. So the possibilities of me getting away from law enforcement were *slim to improbable.* And even if they weren't, where would I go?

I was fortunate though. I noticed Mr. Wright and he spotted me. I don't know how he knew it was me but he was trying his best to steer the Feds from me. It became very clear that they had gotten to the airport sooner than we'd anticipated. Their presence didn't derail my plans to get out of here but they did put a little doubt in my mind that it might just be a little harder to maneuver my way through the terminal.

Meanwhile, the Feds and the airport police were minutes from closing in on me. I tried to

figure out my next step as my heart raced uncontrollably. The edge I had over them was that they were looking for a young woman fitting my description and not a senior citizen woman wearing a grayish colored wig with streaks of black, an old faded blue dress, a pair of orthopedic shoes and walked with a cane. Believe me, I acted the part on queue and used my knowledge of the airport's security system to my advantage. Mr. Wright had hooked me up. Only a select few employees knew the airport was equipped with over a thousand rotating surveillance cameras and fortunately for me, I was one of them. Mr. Wright made sure of that. I also knew there were so many cameras that the security staff could not observe them all simultaneously, which immediately prompted me to change my escape plan.

The airport's generator room was only three feet from me. I eased towards the door very carefully. I acted as if I had lost something on the floor and right before I swiped my key card to make my entry, I glanced around the concourse to make sure I was free and clear. When I realized passengers and airline staff had fixed their attention on the manpower search that had engulfed the entire airport, I knew now was the perfect time to make my exit.

Without hesitation, I swiped my key card and pushed the door open. And just when I thought I was about to make a clean getaway, the security alarm went off. Immediately, my body became panic-stricken. I didn't know whether to proceed through the door or turn back around. But as soon as I heard several of the law enforcement officers yell from behind me, I instinctively looked back and noticed a horde of law enforcement types rapidly rushing towards me. I could tell by the expressions on their faces that they wanted me badly. I slammed the door shut and looked around the machine-filled room for something I could use to barricade the door. My heart beat at an incredible pace as I scanned and moved around the room. Then I finally saw a pipe lying next to one of the big generators. I snatched it up from the floor and said a quiet and quick prayer as I raced back to the door. I heard the commotion on the other side of the door. There were at least two different voices yelling obscenities as they struggled to get the door open.

"Who has a fucking key card?" I heard one officer yell over top of the loud blaring sound of the security alarm.

From that question alone gave me a glimmer of hope that I may be able to prevent them from getting into this room. If I knew Mr. Wright, I was sure he was behind the delay. I knew he wasn't forthcoming with his security badge that accessed this door. Now I had to hurry and place the pipe between the crease of the metal bar and the floor. So when they tried to push the door open, the pipe wouldn't allow the door to move one inch.

Not even ten seconds after I placed the pipe against the door, I heard a loud booming sound hit the door. BOOM! But the door didn't budge. "On the count of three, let's hit it again," I heard one of the officers yell. On the count of three, I watched nervously as they hit the door again. But the door didn't budge. "She's gotta have something barricading the door," I heard another male's voice yell over the top of the continued blaring sounds coming from the alarm system.

Knowing that they had figured out what I had done sent my mind into overdrive. I knew I had very limited time to find my way out of this room before they found a way inside. I had to get a move on it if I wanted to escape this madness.

When I turned around to bolt into the opposite direction, I was stopped in my tracks by a police-issued .40 caliber Glock.

"Where the fuck you think you're going?" said a man's voice as he pointed his pistol directly in my face.

The words *slim to improbable* reverberated throughout my mind as I looked down the biggest barrel I had ever been face-to-face with.

Then my nerves calmed down as Evan my TSA Agent smiled and told me to follow him. I was so surprised to see him. He was supposed to be unloading the plane right now so why was he on the other side of the terminal with me? I needed answers to those questions so I waited until we got to safety before I sprung it on him.

After about five hundred feet of underground tunnels and one man holes, Evan finally got me out of harm's way. It was a feeling of relief when I got into his Ford Expedition and raced away to freedom. At least, I hoped we were racing to freedom.

Chapter 24

Win Some – Lose Some

I had to get myself together mentally after that incident at the airport. It had become a daunting task just to calm my nerves after I took the wig off my head. It seemed like the harder I tried to be optimistic about coming out of this thing altogether, a gut wrenching thought of possibly going to prison may be in the cards for me. The thought of prison life wasn't something I looked forward to. In addition to being arrested, I also thought about how Miguel was going to react when he found out about his shipment. It was clear that it would get confiscated once a thorough investigation was completed. So, I knew I needed to figure out how to ratify that situation as well.

On our way to the city I went into question mode for Evan. I needed some answers. "How did you know where I was? And why did you come for me?" I asked him.

"The airport is tight with security and no one is allowed down in my area of the loading dock but my crew and when I saw a lot of unfamiliar faces show up in the loading area, I knew something was about to go down. So I called my men off the site and sent them to another gate area until I found out what was going on. And when I started asking questions and couldn't get any answers about why they were setting up surveillance in my loading port, I knew your shipment was their target so I switched gears and got out of there."

"Well, how did you know where I was?" I repeated the question.

"I watched you from the time you got off the plane."

"So, why did you save me from them? I mean, if I were you I would've been trying to save myself."

"Naomi, it's gonna come out that me and my men were going to allow that shipment to come in. And when it does, my whole career and retirement is going down the drain. I may be even looking to do some serious time too, so I figured I needed an insurance policy."

Baffled by Evans words, I tried to define his words in laymen terms. I wanted to know what the fuck he was talking about when he said he needed an insurance policy. Then all of a sudden it clicked. He wanted some money from me. A dollar amount hasn't been uttered from his lips, but I knew it was coming next.

I looked back at Evan who happened to be a very small man in statue, but I remembered he mentioned to me some time ago that he worked out at least four days a week. So when I zoomed into the collar area of his shirt, I saw the muscles around his shoulder as clear as day. This Puerto Rican cat would probably have my ass beat up in the back of an alley real bad if I didn't give him what he wanted. He has been an associate of mines for a long time and he had been loyal to me, so I guess he figured it was time for him to cash out and go off on his own. Clearly it was every man for himself.

Pretending to stay calm, I said, "What kind of an insurance policy are we talking about?"

"For where I am going, I am going to need five hundred thousand dollars." he said and he did not blink one eye nor did his expression change. This guy acted like he was dead serious.

I thought for a moment about how much money I had back at my place. I knew that it wasn't near the amount he asked for but I hoped that it would help by me some time. "Evan, I don't have five hundred grand at my disposal. But I can get at least one hundred and fifty of it to you."

Evan slammed his fist on the steering wheel. "No!" he roared. "That's not enough. I want five hundred thousand dollars right now. Now if you can't get it to me, then you and I are going to go on a very long ride Chica."

After I watched Evan snap out like he'd just done, I got a whole new sense of reality. This guy wasn't stable at all and I had the slightest clue as to what to do next.

"You better think of something real quick because I'm trying to be out of town in the next couple of hours." he concluded.

"Can I make a phone call?" I asked.

"Hell, no! I'm not stupid. You'll try to get me ambushed."

"So, how do you expect me to get the rest of the money for you?"

"Get it from your bank account. I know you gotta have some of it there."

My heart continued to race and my mind wouldn't unscramble my thoughts. I thought I was about to lose my fucking mind. I figured what in the hell could go wrong next? But then it came to me, that I was instructed to go by our hideaway spot. Damian insisted that he'd meet me there so that's where I decided to take Evan. Until this very moment, I liked Evan. He was indeed a soldier for our operation, but don't bite the hand that fed you all this time. That's a fucking no-no! And when it was all said and done, one of his loved ones would need his insurance policy.

"I can't go to my bank. That's too risky. Take me to my apartment at 145 West 67th Street. I got a drop off I was supposed to deposit in the bank yesterday. There's more than enough in there for you to get your share and for me to take and leave town with." I said.

"Oh no way, Chica. I'm getting everything you got. I put my neck on the line for you. You owe me for all those times you underpaid me for helping you to bring in your fucking drugs." he growled, his facial expression got more menacing.

I remained calm. I knew something he didn't; his life was coming to a screeching halt when Damian found out that he intended to rob us. Talk about a sad ending.

As we approached the apartment building, I searched both sides of the block to see if I noticed Reggie or Damian's cars parked anywhere, but I didn't. The optimism of getting Evan off my back dissipated rapidly. Fear crept right back into my heart at that very moment because I knew that I would have to fight this battle all by myself. I started to stall him, but I knew that would only piss him off so I climbed out of the truck and made my way up to the apartment while Evan followed.

I fumbled with the key at the front door so he snatched the keys away from me and unlocked it himself. Immediately after he opened up the front door, he pushed me inside but instructed me to stand where he could see me. And before he made his entrance, he peeped around the door to make sure the coast was clear with his gun cocked and ready to fire. I stood there and faced him head on trying to figure out how I would handle this situation. "Now, let's get that money." he said and then he turned his back to shut the front door behind himself. Having him turn his back on me gave me a big enough window to make a run for Reggie's room so I could grab his money bag and hop out of the window. But all plans don't go as they were mapped out because as soon as I turned to dip in the opposite direction, I was startled by Reggie himself. It all happened so quickly. Reggie pressed his hand against my mouth to keep me from screaming and then he pushed me off to the side. And as soon as Evan turned around, he realized that he had a standoff with the head boss of our operation. Evan had never met Reggie, so he never knew what he looked like. But, I guessed he was about to find out. "Look, all I want is what's owed to me." Evan said as he kept close to the front door.

"I don't owe you shit. You came here to rob us." I spat.

"Nigga, you came here to rob me and my sister?" Reggie roared as he pointed his pistol with his silencer attached towards Evan.

"No, she promised to pay me for the load that came in today. And I'm trying to leave town so I need my money." Evan continued as he looked at me and Reggie both. He seemed like he was getting a little scared.

"What load nigga? We didn't have a load to come in today." Reggie challenged him. I knew he was playing head games with Evan. Reggie wasn't about to admit to having no involvement with Miguel's load whatsoever. Reggie was the type of cat that he wouldn't admit to doing shit even if you caught him in the act.

"I'm talking about that load that Naomi had me and my boys to offload from the plane. But we couldn't do it because the FEDS came in and intercepted it."

"So, that means you couldn't do your job right?" Reggie pressed on.

"We tried. Bu......but.....we couldn't." Evan tried to explain but he started stuttering his words.

"That's too bad." Reggie said and without warning he pulled the trigger and shot Evan twice in the face. Evan's body fell back against the door and made a loud thud noise. Blood splattered the back of the door and on the walls nearby. I swear I couldn't believe my eyes.

"Why the fuck you bring him here?" Reggie questioned me. I knew he was pissed. But I had no other choice.

"Trust me I didn't mean to. He saw me trying to get away from the FEDS at the airport and helped me. And then when we got into his truck, he started acting crazy and threatening to do shit to me if I didn't give him five hundred grand. I tried to settle with him by giving him the one hundred and fifty grand at my place but he wouldn't take it. So, what was I supposed to do? Let him kill me."

"Come on and help me move this nigga out of the way. Damian and Stone should be here in a minute." he said. I thought he would've answered my question. But he didn't. I guess he figured that I didn't have a choice after all.

We grabbed a box of industrial size trash bags we used to wrap our money in and took it to the where Evan's body had laid. But before we touched him he slipped on plastic gloves and a surgical mask.

"Help me grab his legs first." Reggie instructed me. The bags we had were big enough to put a human who was 5'5 or shorter inside of it. And since Evan was right there at that height, his body fitted the bag perfectly. I believed we covered him in at least ten bags. And when we were done we wrapped gray electric tape around his waist and we sealed the top of it with the same tape. Reggie made sure we contained the rest of his blood and the odor that comes from a dead corpse.

Immediately afterwards, I struggled to get up all Evan's blood that soaked into the carpet before we moved his body into the bathroom shower. I used ammonia, bleach and baking soda and when I realized that this wouldn't do the trick I grabbed a pair of utility scissors from the kitchen and cut the entire area of the blood stained carpet and removed it from the floor. I asked Reggie what to do with it and he simply said,

"Lay it on top of that nigga in the tub. I'll get Stone and Damian to take it out when they get him."

"Alright," I said and then I went on and finished the task at hand.

Now while I cleaned up behind myself and made sure that everything I used to dispose of Evan's body with was thrown into another trash bag, Reggie was in the other room gathering up his things. I heard him counting all the money his money. And then I heard him fumbling with something in his closet. I didn't bother him because I knew he needed this time to figure out our next step, so I made a detour into my room and gathered up my things as well.

Chapter 25

The Last Man Standing

Fifteen minutes later Damian and Stone finally showed up. Stone was ready to walk back out the door the moment he stepped inside. He made it blatantly obvious that he was ready to get us out of there. "Come on, let's go. I got my other driver outside waiting for us." he told us. But after Reggie ran down what happened before they got there, Stone wasn't pleased to hear that he had to dispose of a body while it's still broad daylight. "You know I'll die for you Reggie. But, that would be a dumb move to move that body while it's still daylight. We're gonna have to change plans."

"Nah, we can't do that. It's gonna fuck up everything." Reggie argued.

Stone wouldn't stand down. He was adamant about handling his business a certain way. "I'm sorry. But, I won't do it," he told Reggie.

Reggie wasn't used to hearing someone telling him no. He was the boss and he always had the last say in any situation. "Look, Stone you know I don't like changing plans. That motherfucker came to us with his bullshit. So, we had to deal with it accordingly. And if we hadn't and allowed him to go free then the cops would've been all over us right now."

Damian and I sat there across from each other and waited to see how this thing with Stone and Reggie would play out. We knew we needed to get out of there but we also knew that we couldn't leave until the body was gone first.

"Why don't y'all leave now and I'll catch up to you later on tonight." Stone suggested.

"But we're gonna need you to drive. That was the plan. Remember?"

"Yeah, that was the plan until I found out you got a dead body lying back there in the damn bathtub."

Damian saw that this ordeal with Reggie and Stone wouldn't be resolved as quickly as we'd liked, so he stood up and said, "Why don't we all stay here until nightfall and then we make a run for it?"

"Nah, that's a dumbass plan. Our faces will be plastered all over the fucking TV by then. Not to mention, the neighbors in this building knows how we look. Don't you think they'll blow the whistle on us for some fucking reward money if the FEDS say their offering it?"

"He's got a point Damian." I said.

"But what other choice do you have?" Stone chimed in.

"I say we blow this joint now. I got a duffle bag filled with dough that'll last me for a while. And all I need for you to do is get me across the Mexico Border so I can chill out over there for a few months until this shit blows over. By that time, Vanessa will have let her guard down and brought her stinky ass out of hiding and then boom, I could've snuck back into the states without anyone knowing and have that bitch carved up like a pig on a silver platter."

"And what do we do in the meantime?" I spoke up. I realized that none of Reggie's plans included me or Damian.

"Right now sis, we gotta go our separate ways. It wouldn't be a good look to have all of us going to the same place. We can meet up sometime later though."

"You can go with me out west if you like." Damian suggested to me. I knew what he was doing. So, I played it off and went along with him.

"Are you sure?" I asked.

"Yeah, I'm sure. That way I can keep an eye on you and make sure you're safe." he continued.

"Stop the bullshit you two!" Reggie yelled. "I know what's going on. I know y'all fucking. So, cut it out."

"What!" I said, trying to act like I was shocked.

"What, nothing. I've noticed how y'all been acting towards each other lately. I can tell how a nigga acts after he gets the pussy."

"Come on now Reggie, not now." Damian tried to defuse the conversation.

"Whatcha mean not now?" Reggie turned his attention towards Damian, "Trust me nigga, I could care less about what y'all are doing. Just don't try to play me like I'm some stupid ass nigga from around the way."

"Ain't nobody trying to play you dawg. Out of respect for you, I just wanna make sure Naomi is alright. That's all."

Meanwhile Stone's cell phone rings and after he answered it, his facial expression changed. "Alright. We'll handle it on this end." he told the caller and then he hung up. "My guy outside just informed me that about eight FBI Agents just hopped out of their cars and that they're trying to get into the building right now."

"Oh shit!" I said as my body was instantly struck with fear. I rushed back to my bedroom, grabbed my duffle bag from the bed and dashed back into the front room. Reggie had already bolted out of the front door but Damian stood there and waited for me. He extended his hand and said, "Come on baby," let's go."

I took his hand and followed him out the front door. I had no idea where the hell he planned to take me so I resisted a little, "Didn't Stone say they were trying to come through the front door, so where are we going?"

"Reggie said that there was an underground utility basement in the laundry room on the first floor, so we're going down the back staircase to get there."

"What about Stone? What is he going to do?" I continued to question him.

"Don't worry about him. He's going to be fine. He said he'll meet up with us in a few minutes." Damian explained and then he literally pulled me forcibly down the stairway.

When we reached the bottom floor, Damian heard a loud BOOM. Then the building shook. Debris from the ceiling started falling down around us. Visions of me dying inside of this building engulfed me and my body became numb. But that didn't stop Damian. He dragged me into the laundry room and down the stairs that lead to the basement. The door had already been kicked open by Reggie, so we knew we weren't that far behind him.

The basement was poorly lit with old light bulbs but that didn't deter us from finding our way out of there. The thought of freedom weighed heavy on my heart. I wanted it so badly I could taste it. So, I held onto Damian's hand and helped him, help me get to freedom.

"Come on baby, we're almost there." he said. And when I zoomed in ahead of us and noticed that there was indeed light at the end of this tunnel, I began to breathe. The weight of everything around me fell off my shoulders as we approached the half cracked doorway that lead to the outside. And when we finally wiggled our way through it and was able to see that the coast was clear, we fled on foot away from the building and hoped that we'd flag down a cab before the FBI got wind of which direction we ran.

I can't lie, I was dead tired, exhausted to say the least. Reggie was nowhere in sight and that frightened me. But what really frightened me was when I looked back at the building, I noticed that the apartment we had and the entire floor had blown up and was completely engulfed in flames. My heart sunk at the thought that Stone had started an explosion in the apartment and killed himself in the process so that we could getaway. This was something you'd see in a fucking movie. There was no way I would've done that for anyone else. Nor did I have the guts to even attempt something of that magnitude. Stone gave new meaning to the word loyalty. And he'll be forever in my heart.

We walked a total of five blocks before we caught a cab. And instead of telling the cab driver to take us to the nearest transit station, we told him to take us north towards Connecticut. Thank God he didn't ask us any questions. But he required us to give him cash up front before he moved the car, so we did. And as soon as the cab pulled back on the road and began to head north, Damian and I were finally able to let out a long sigh.

EPILOGUE

It had been two weeks since Damian and I left New York. We've traveled from state to state and stayed out of the public eye. It took about five days before we saw our faces broadcasted on national television so I panicked the first time I saw it. But Damian reminded me that as long as we had our fake passports and driver's licenses on hand, then we were fine.

Periodically, I'd worry about what was going on back in New York. The thought of not being able to speak to my parents bothered me more than not knowing where Reggie was because I knew he could take care of himself. And since there were no new reports about him getting arrested, I knew he was still on the streets. My guess was that he'd be sitting on a beach somewhere, sipping on a cold Corona with a slice of lime floating at the top of the bottle. But when my brand new cell phone rung I got an entirely different story.

Damian was sitting next to me on the hotel bed when the call came through. He and I both looked at each other like we'd just saw a ghost. "Hello," I said, after allowing the phone to ring four times.

"Hey sis, this is your brother." Reggie yelled through the phone.

His voice magnified with each word he uttered. He sounded like he was excited about something. But I was even more excited to hear his voice and to know that he was alright. “Oh my God! I can’t believe it’s you.” I said and then I pressed the speaker phone button so Damian could hear our conversation.

“Yeah, it’s me. So, I guess y’all are alright?” he yelled again. There was a lot of loud traffic noise in the back ground so I assumed he was either walking or driving with the windows down, which made it very hard for him to hear me.

“Yeah, we’re good. And you?”

“Yeah, I’m great. I’m still roaming around the city. I couldn’t bring myself to leave after I found out what Stone did for us. Plus, I wasn’t going to let Vanessa off the hook after what she did to me. She basically destroyed everything I built.”

I placed my hand over my mouth. “Reggie, what did you do?” I forced myself to say.

“Let’s just say that she won’t be running her fucking mouth anymore. I got her, that nigga Ben and that nigga Dre torched in a house fire. They thought I wasn’t gonna find out they were hiding out at Ben’s sister’s house in the Bronx.”

Shocked by his words, I said, “What!”

Reggie chuckled. “Yeah, I paid that nigga that Stone had waiting for us outside, to put me up in his crib for a while. Then I got him to help me find out where those motherfuckers were hiding out. And instead of running in the crib and blasting all of them in their fucking heads, me and that cat decided to close off all the windows, barricade the front door and set the spot on fire so we could burn them alive. You should’ve heard Vanessa screaming when that fire got to her ass. It was like music to my ears.”

“Vanessa’s dead?”

"Damn right! That bitch and those niggas finally got what they deserved."

"So, what do we do now?" I asked him. Believe it or not, Damian and I needed a plan. I was tired of going from one hotel to the next. And I was sure Damian felt the same way.

"I don't know what to tell you right now. But I do know that coming back to New York isn't the answer because Marco and Miguel are standing in line behind the FEDS, so they are looking for us too."

I didn't want to admit it, but I knew there was a chance that Marco would have us on his radar after we lost his shipment to the FEDS. So, there's another situation we had to handle. "What about mom and dad? Have you been able to see or talk to them?" I asked.

"No I haven't. But I've been able to get money to them though. So don't worry, they're in good hands."

"So, what's next for you?"

"I don't know baby sis. But I do know that I can't leave New York right now especially with all the product we have left. I talked to Stone's people and they've agreed to help me get rid of all that's left. So, until that mission is completed, I'm a sitting duck."

"Don't you think that's a little too risky?"

"Of course it is. But, what am I going to do with one and a half million dollars' worth of product? Just let it sit in the warehouse and collect dusk. No way. I'm a businessman. And besides that, I got a baby on the way. I couldn't leave Malika either."

"Sounds like you got a lot on your plate." I said.

He chuckled again. "Yeah, it looks that way doesn't it?"

I wanted to answer him but I couldn't because I realized that I was losing him to the world of drugs. Like my dad Foxx, Reggie was born and raised in that whole scene so it was a part of his DNA and no one would be able to get him to walk away from it. Now it was a matter of life or death.

"Hey listen baby sis, tell Damian I said to take care of you. A'ight?"

"Alright," I managed to say, my voice started cracking.

"Oh yeah, and I want you to know that if you ever get word that something happened to me, don't start crying and shit. Just get yourself together and bring your ass back to the city because I'm gonna have a large amount of cash put away for you and my unborn child. You follow me?"

"Yeah, but how will I know where to find it?"

"Just think back to where we used to play when we were kids. And when you remember the spot, then you'll know where to go from there. Now, I gotta go. I love you."

"I love you too." I assured him and then our call ended.

I sat there on the bed and wondered how my life would play out. I knew I didn't want it to play out in jail and I also knew that I didn't want to end up dead, so I looked at Damian and said, "Do you promise to keep me safe?"

And his reply was, "What kind of question is that? Of course I will."

COMING SOON

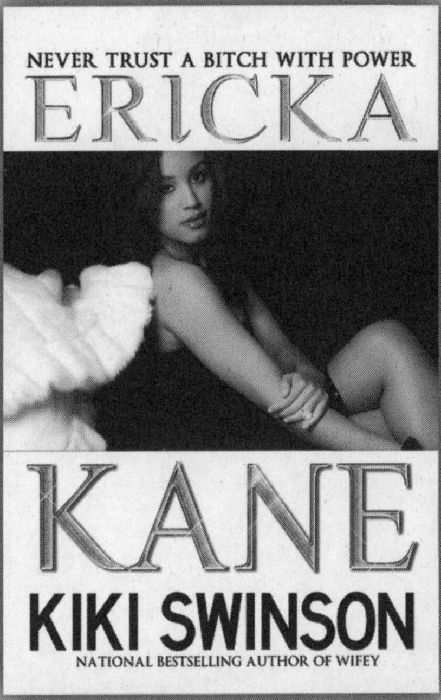
NEVER TRUST A BITCH WITH POWER
ERICKA
KANE
KIKI SWINSON
NATIONAL BESTSELLING AUTHOR OF WIFEY

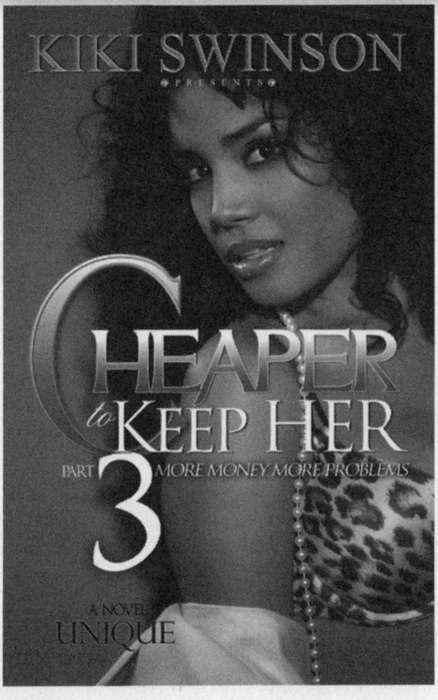
KIKI SWINSON
PRESENTS
CHEAPER to KEEP HER
PART 3
MORE MONEY MORE PROBLEMS
A NOVEL
UNIQUE

COMING SOON

WIFE
Extraordinaire
RETURNS
[PART 2]
KiKi Swinson
ESSENCE® BESTSELLING AUTHOR OF WIFEY

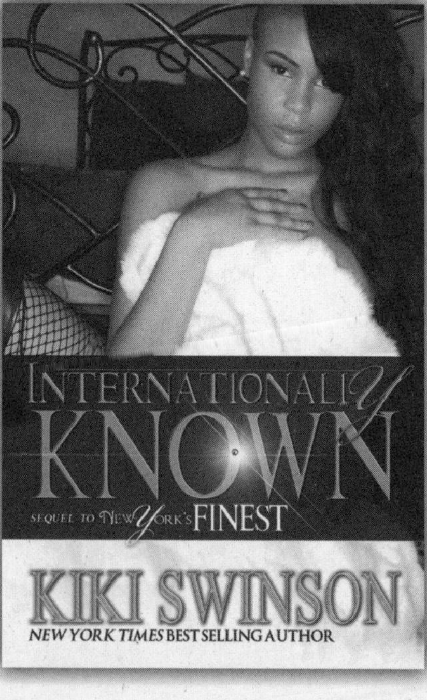
INTERNATIONALLY
KNOWN
SEQUEL TO NEW YORK'S FINEST
KIKI SWINSON
NEW YORK TIMES BEST SELLING AUTHOR